THE JOHN HARVARD LIBRARY

The John Harvard Library, founded in 1959, publishes essential American writings, including novels, poetry, memoirs, criticism, and works of social and political history, representing all periods, from the beginning of settlement in America to the twenty-first century. The purpose of The John Harvard Library is to make these works available to scholars and general readers in affordable, authoritative editions.

T. D. RICE

JIM CROW, AMERICAN

Selected Songs and Plays

EDITED BY W. T. LHAMON, JR.

THE BELKNAP PRESS OF HARVARD UNIVERSITY PRESS

Cambridge, Massachusetts, and London, England 2009

Library of Congress Cataloging-in-Publication Data

Jim Crow, American : selected songs and plays / T. D. Rice / edited by W. T. Lhamon, Jr.
p.   cm.—(John Harvard library)
Includes bibliographical references.
ISBN 978-0-674-03593-5 (alk. paper)
1. Rice, Tom, 1808–1860.   2. Minstrel shows—United States—History.
3. Blackface entertainers—United States—History.   4. Minstrel music.
5. Tricksters—United States—History—19th century.   I. Lhamon, W. T., Jr.
PN1969.M5J56   2009
791'.12'0973—dc22   2009022920

Contents

Introduction: Dis United State vii

Note on the Text xxv

Chronology xxix

SONGS

"The Original Jim Crow" 2

"Jim Crow, Still Alive!!!" 9

"De Original Jim Crow" 27

"Jim Crow" 30

"Clare de Kitchen" 36

v

"Gombo Chaff"   38

"Sich a Gitting Up Stairs"   41

"Jim Crack Corn, or the Blue Tail Fly"   42

"Settin' on a Rail, or, Racoon Hunt"   44

PLAYS

Virginia Mummy   48

Bone Squash   71

Otello   110

ILLUSTRATIONS

Otello playbill, Cincinnati National Theatre (May 9, 1846)   xxi

"Mr. T. Rice as the Original Jim Crow," by Edward Williams
    Clay   57

"A Dead Cut," from the series *Life in Philadelphia*, by Edward
    Williams Clay   85

Notes   161

Selected Bibliography   185

Introduction: Dis United State

When we discover the early songs and plays about Jim Crow, we find a past surprisingly awry from its received history. Reading the plays and singing the songs in our minds, we overhear members of America's second cultural generation assessing dilemmas that were determining them. We soon realize that those dilemmas, unresolved after two centuries, work their way on us still.

What was different in the 1830s was that Antebellum Americans were just beginning to assemble images sufficiently complex to contain and sustain their problems. Thirty years before Emancipation, racial anxiety was stirring in ways that started the long breakdown of North American slavery. Some slaves were successful runaways. Northern statutes and uncertain masters in every region manumitted others. Even when slaves remained in bonds, they resisted in the countless ways of people who have no stake. Thus, in tightening its grip, the "peculiar institution" of slavery was also losing it. Stark gradients of freedom and its opposite were startlingly loose, together, on the land. Much of what condensed these disparities into the diagnostic consciousness of Americans has been the unsettling image of a ragged black man, dancing on his broken bonds, sassing his antagonists, and rousing publics both black and white. You could cheer him on and you could loathe his action. He represented the issue as it bore down on everyone. He figured it out.

Before the late 1820s, the figure of Jim Crow was current chiefly among blacks, who performed him as a folk trickster. During this earliest phase of his maturation, he was an agent for tribal Africans exploring their black mutualities within American unfreedom, after the middle passage. A second phase occurred during the 1830s and early 1840s, when Jim Crow became an icon over which political forces agreed to struggle. After that, in a lasting third phase, Jim Crow came to name the nation's segregated shame. Contrary meanings piled on Jim Crow as everyone tried to promote or police his signals.

The crucial middle phase—the 1830s and 1840s—is what *Jim Crow, American* reckons. During this interval, working white audiences adapted the early black knowledge of the crow as trickster, championed it, and brought it into general recognition as a sign of their own disaffection. During this thaw between firm meanings, "Jim Crow" was a dervish on low stages dancing and singing the early Republic's scary vernacular energy. To read the scripts that incorporated him is to enter a history of disaffected emotion unavailable by any other means. These scripts long ago compressed sufficient power to display, and presently diagnose, America's distinctive agony. By following the development of these plays for just a decade and a half we also see hatching the central drama of America's popular culture. That drama is the struggle between the welling of inclusive democracy and a clampdown that excludes it. We see developing the moral and performance panics that this struggle has since generated at regular intervals. *Tick*: minstrelsy; *tock*: ragtime; *tick*: blues; *tock*: jazz; *tick*: rhythm 'n' blues; *tock*: rock 'n' roll; *tick*: punk; *tock*: hip-hop—and that simply lists the gross cogs on one of this cultural pattern's escapements.

By adapting previous trickster figures active in black folklore, white and black song-and-dance men working in and out of blackface laid down cultural templates that brought people of every hue into troubled relation. As Abraham Lincoln noted in his early Lyceum speech, this was the generation coming up after the Republic's Founders had passed. Epochal momentum reached cruising speed by the 1830s. The era's songs and plays came in time to influence—perhaps determine—the American Renaissance just before the Civil War. Its public understood that Jim Crow's insouciance tokened the new underclass aggression that multitudes sought and the middle class feared in theater and literature, painting and music.

If American plays enact distinctively American topics that are significant in every region and find formal verve to match their material, then the Jim Crow scripts are the country's earliest. If raking the country's rawest nerves counts, these plays contend for the nineteenth century's best. Like other successful interventions, they arrive terse and develop as they go. Ultimately ambiguous, the better to gather conflicting needs, they still know where the rub is. Their provocations are sure. By enacting and showing how to burst every political and cultural bond, they speak for unincluded Americans—for those not yet franchised. Thus, these scripts organize and launch their era's new publics, confirming their affiliations. Jim Crow wheels about in these plays, advocating abolition, nixing secession, pushing black pride. He notes where he is barred, where included. He shoves white and black dandies equally hard, talks street jive, mocks elite notions of class and history, courts ladies, treats gents. Jim Crow acts out these topics, rarely discoursing on anything. His dodgy repartee points to the clown and dizzard. He deals in the slippery modes that unequal people practice in public places. He avoids the muscular declamation of a star facing front from the footlights that melodrama favored in the era before Jim Crow overtook the stage. He replaces neither melodrama nor the pretense that it occurs in a society of equals, but he enlivens a lasting, sneaky alternative to it. Thus Jim Crow's volatility was unprecedented on the Republic's main stages because he erupted there from low vernacular performance.

Anyone raised during the American "one-drop" eras—one drop of black blood and you were black—will be surprised to find that the first Atlantic popular culture smudged that binary with a vengeance. These Jim Crow scripts reveal no race *line* beyond which a person is one category or its opposite. Rather, they show a wide *threshold* chocked with attraction and joint positions. Whiteness and blackness tangle there, knotting together so inextricably that their separation seems a mad fantasy. Their overlap could be symbolic: actors covering visible skin in burnt cork to try out being black. The urge could come from the other edge of the threshold, too, as when slaves in the Tidewater regions tried out Euro-derived steps, supplementing them with moves they brought from Africa, their combine becoming "Jigs."[1] Later, ragtime dancers, often blacks in blackface, enhanced white operatic with streetwise strutting. They called it "cakewalking." And overlap could be literal: Desdemona explained in *Otello* (included in this volume) why she "loved the Black." Hearing his storied prowess, she swooned. When she awoke, she was not only "sitting on his knee" but pregnant. She called that result—and the carefully handwritten script punned it—"Greatful."

These entanglements demonstrate that struggles over race in the United States have always been as much about championing as outlawing black allure. The prohibition developed, of course, because the celebration came first. The laws intending to disintegrate Jim Crow manifested their crazed necessity only because his impulse to integrate was primary and vital. And the very beginning of figuring out this vitality came not from whites at all but from North American blacks themselves, during the eighteenth and early nineteenth centuries. African Americans performed Jim Crow energetically on their own well before his name was known among whites. He was never a real person. Rather, he was a fractious spirit, sneaky, a bit beyond good or evil, whose storied provenance rose from rites of song and dance. In the Georgia Sea Islands, and elsewhere, too, Jim Crow was a winking phrase rehearsed regularly about an advance man who scavenged newly cleared territory.

Might we hazard more about this crow who fascinated rural slaves before he became popular among savvy European immigrants? There was a John Crow, whom many people from the Caribbean up to the Carolinas called the buzzard, and there was a Jim Crow, familiar in all the Atlantic as our raucous, sociable scavenger.[2] John and Jim Crow poached the very edge of cleared ground before returning, mumbling, sometimes screeching, about what it was like out there. They were twisted. What they experienced made them as difficult to accommodate as the corn gods of Mediterranean and European lores. Jim Crow is the American Osiris, whom Ishmael Reed enlisted in *Mumbo Jumbo*. Reed recognized the Egyptian corn god as the "man who did dances that caught-on."[3] Jim Crow is the American Lear, rejected and therefore opened to the renewal of the corn. In the climactic act of *King Lear*, Cordelia notes that her father is "Crown'd with . . . all the idle weeds that grow / In our sustaining corn" (3.4.3–6). When he enters, "bedecked with weeds," his insight peaks about the way people perform themselves: "they cannot touch me for coining," he says. "I am the King himself" (3.6.83–84). Jim Crow never pretended to be king, but he coined himself in every low aspect. The devil in *Bone*

Squash Diavolo tells him, "you're like a 'lasses candy in a shop window. You run away all sides" (2.2). And Ginger Blue's last words in *Virginia Mummy* rival Lear's awareness of life's determined roles: "should any ob de faculty hab occasion for a libe mummy again, dey hab only to call on Ginger Blue; when dey'll find him ready dried, smoked, and painted, to sarbe himself up at de shortest notice."

That connection across disparate lores is one of Jim Crow's continuing meanings. He blends diverse peoples' backgrounds. Both early black and early white performers of Jim Crow link him to cornfields, corn cobs, corn fiddles, corn shucking, and cornmeal. The 1830 newspaper reviews of the Jim Crow stage character, casually racist, called him a "cornfield nigger" and understood him to represent deep truths either unavailable to, or abandoned by, his metrosexual antagonist, Zip Coon. In the 1840s, Dan Emmett coded Jim Crow's meaning in his famous chorus: "Jim crack corn I don't care, / Ole Massa gone away." The crow finally, Emmett fantasied then, had access to life's resources. When hierarchy had passed, full democracy might flourish and powerless people crack, like Lear, their ultimate corn. But who today understands the song like that? Instead of incorporating Jim Crow's tricky complexity, America warped his meanings while continuing to spin out the gestures that perplex us even unto our own era.

As late as 1972, a black resident of the Georgia Sea Islands talked about the Jim Crow gyrations she had danced since a child: "When I was a little girl, I thought Jim Crow might have been a bird, because it was 'going down to the new ground,' and they always shoot them birds out of the corn. 'New ground' is ground where the trees have been cut off, but it's never been planted in. So that was what I understood at the time, that was my idea. But we don't know what the old folks meant, we sure don't."[4]

She delivers "Knock Jim Crow" this way:

> Where you going buzzard?
> Where you going, crow?
> I'm going down to new ground
> To knock Jim Crow.

A century and a half before she wondered what Jim Crow "might have been," several itinerant performers, black and white, adapted that old song to the wider performance that industrial and metropolitan modes were making possible early in the nineteenth century.

Foremost among these imitators was Thomas Dartmouth Rice, a white actor in a traveling troupe who came to bill himself "Jim Crow" Rice. Here are lyrics from one of his earliest printed variants of "Jump Jim Crow":

> I neeld to de buzzard
> An I bou'd to de Crow
> an eb'ry time I reel'd
> Why I jump't Jim Crow.
> (1832, Harvard Theatre Collection)

Rice's "Jump Jim Crow" song retained the folk imagery and fascination with the crow's trouble, but he inhabited that trouble rather than knocking it away. "Jump Jim Crow" went into its own new ground furthering the figure's spin.

The "Jim Crow" lyrics deserve a book by themselves. They mushroom into a shifty zone that matches their own mercurial improvisation. They were printed, and thus would seem to be nailed down, but publishing only goosed along their change. Rather than attaching him to positions, the way media today clasp a politician or an author to an utterance, publishing these songs proliferated their conflicts. Jim Crow could refer, for instance, to a "nigger" in ways already and every bit as demeaning as our current parlance—and already also showing our contemporary term's meaning of brotherhood. He fertilized exact contraries in the same verse. Here are three consecutive stanzas from another early printed version of "Jump Jim Crow":

> Should dey get to fighting,
> Perhaps de blacks will rise,
> For deir wish for freedom,
> Is shining in deir eyes.
>
> An if de blacks should get free,
> I guess dey'll fee some bigger,
> An I shall concider it,
> A bold stroke for de niggar.
>
> I'm for freedom,
> An for Union altogether,
> Aldough I'm a black man,
> De white is call'd my broder.

This zest for conflict is undoubtedly one of the most important aspects of Jim Crow. He, like the public that was finding itself around his performances, encouraged the complex and contrary racial formations stirring well before Emancipation—and hastened its decree.

The son of a ship's rigger in New York City's poorest area, the ethnically mixed Seventh Ward, Rice learned to dance at Catharine Market, along the wharves where sailors caroused, where black truck farmers—some still enslaved to owners in Brooklyn—danced out cutting contests on shingles for small change and, sometimes, for eels. Rice watched them all. He apprenticed as a ship's carver but early abandoned that craft for the theater. Nineteenth-century stage memoirists recall Rice as a youngster at a rude theater on Cherry Lane, near the rough neighborhood of Five Points, where he probably grew up. About 1828, when he would have turned twenty, he appeared as a supernumerary stealing scenes from the seasoned players at the tony Park Theater. When the leading players complained of the applause Rice was winning, he moved to lower venues, the Lafayette and Chatham. There he played the comic roles of his era's repertoire, all inherited from England, most concerning capers among the squire-archy.

Late in 1828, Rice joined Noah Ludlow's troupe, sailing from New York down around Florida and coming into what was then the West at Mobile. He would tour the Mississippi and Ohio valleys for the next two years. After Ludlow, Tom Rice also worked with Sam Drake (who had alternated between Saratoga Springs and America's out-posts for more than a decade) and with Purdy Brown's Circus and Equestrian Theater. Rice leapt from one troupe to the other as they occupied, and lost, halls and theaters. In Pensacola's Tivoli, Cincin-nati's Amphi-Theater, Louisville's Melo-Dramatic and City theaters, Rice performed comic dances before the curtain while stagehands scurried to change sets behind it. When the curtain rose, his roles were the provokers of rough noise and quick-changing servants, the clowns always underfoot and in your face.

Gradually during those years, Rice's dances morphed from reels to wheels—from Tom and Jerry toward Jim Crow. This change was the first significant phase in the performance makeover he was assem-bling for the New World. In Louisville, in early April and early May 1830, Rice sang "Coal Black Rose," probably in blackface. That means he was moving toward "Jump Jim Crow" even before he first plugged it into a play that Sam Drake adapted from a short story by the New York journalist William Leggett. His insertion was not accidental nor whimsical. It was not the result of a chance meeting with a pitiful stable hand, as many legends insist. It was a concerted effort to move into new territory. The date was May 21, 1830. "Jump Jim Crow" was his way to cackle at the hypocrisy already apparent just one genera-tion after the Declaration of Independence had promised that equal-ity was "self-evident."

The story that would first carry the song "Jump Jim Crow" was it-self sliding like the song. The script for its play is now lost, but we can discover many of its elements from Leggett's story, its newspaper ads and reviews, and the development of the song it made famous. Leg-gett had set his 1928 story in his native Illinois. Sam Drake and Tom Rice changed the title from "The Rifle" to "The Kentucky Rifle," and Drake billed Rice's lyrics a "Kentucky Corn Song." They wanted to bring it home from prairie to plantation and drench it in the mad blackness of the corn. However skewed and crude Jim Crow was as a representation of black manhood, he was neither head-scratchingly deferential nor ashamed of himself. He was free, brash, thriving on his wits. None of this—indeed, nothing black—had been in Leggett's original story. It had dealt only with frontiersmen framing for mur-der an honest young doctor courting a maiden in her prime, all uni-formly white. The insertion of Rice's blackface figure interrupted Leggett's plot. This decentering spin diverted attention from the old story, as Rice had always done, but now he was learning to occupy the vacuum, leaping into the gasp that followed on his action.

Drake's ad in the Louisville *Public Advertiser* called *The Kentucky Rifle* "home-bred," a "native morceau." He contrasted the play with the English melodramas and faux-classical fragments then still squat-ting in the theater of the early Republic. But jabbing this black rogue into the American imagination turned out revolutionary because its popularity correctly embodied and named elements obsessing Amer-ican culture. Now they had tags that focused consideration. Such in-sertion is also the way T. D. Rice made his plays. He brought blackness in the house by injecting extant white tales of varied quality—from "The Rifle" to *Othello*—with unavoidable black charisma.

At first the integrator had not fully emerged from the old stereotype. In *The Kentucky Rifle* Rice's character singing about Jim Crow was still named Sambo. He had only enough allure to assert his presence for the moment. Over the next few years, Rice firmed up the figure. He first expanded "Jump Jim Crow" into shifting, topical extravaganzas some hundred stanzas long. Then he created narrative contexts to house his energy. He completed the pattern by the spring of 1835, with the opening of *Virginia Mummy* in Mobile. Rice altered a two-year-old English farce, *The Mummy*, by William Bayle Bernard (an American writing in London). Adaptation consisted here of integrating Ginger Blue, a new character dumb as Brer Rabbit, into the old plot. The banter comes as fast as the scenes change, and black Ginger gives better than he gets. So much so that his new employer confesses early that "the rascal seems to be between the two—cunning as well as stupid." This employer will recognize too late, after Ginger has maneuvered him off stage and performed the pass from one era to another, that seeming stupid can be cunning's cardinal feature.

In addition to the daily abuse that even free blacks like Ginger endured in slavery times, he must suffer stock twits of other ethnicities mocking him. He must play dead. He fears that the mad scientist will drill his brain and poison him. He must contend with people trying to bite and slice off his digits. Despite these morbid fears, the clear point of the play is that he is not victim but victor. He outwits every antagonist or fights back physically, head-butting and kicking when necessary, thus rendering them ridiculous. After Ginger kicks one antagonist, that character runs off stage, shouting, "Murther! murther!— I'm kilt! I'm kilt by a dead man." Significantly, the audience applauds Ginger's self-reliance. His inventiveness in fighting hypocritical constraint manifests the audience's own fantasy.

Rice then followed this same insertion strategy in *Bone Squash Diavolo* but doubled the target. His title mocked Daniel Auber's opera

Fra Diavolo, popular in London in 1830. Then he named this play's black invader "Bone Squash" to sport with *Beau Nash* (1834), Douglas Jerrold's London hit about a gambling rake. The scene in *Bone Squash Diavolo* elaborates a conflicted black urbanity, replete with boot blacks and barbers, a duck-legged minister and his aspiring daughter, dandies, chimney sweeps, musicians, and more. The play has but one white character among all the blacks. He suddenly emerges, from maroon fires and a crashing gong, in the form of the Devil, a seemingly indomitable force dispensing checks to buy up souls. The black characters must repel him to restore their ragged life. But devils who own your soul, Bone finds predictably enough, do not retire easily. Less predictable is that the help of a sympathetic chorus and chaotic spectacle not seen before on the American stage checks that white Devil, drops him down whence he came, and raises Bone to his cornfield charisma. This explosive form does not punish Bone's lumpen desires or cut off his future; just the opposite. Least predictable of all is that Bone's defeat of the Devil sets a template for American second starts that will run from Hester Prynne to Ishmael, from Faulkner's Flem Snopes to Ralph Ellison's invisible man. After runaway slaves persisting against all odds, nothing seems more American than starting over. Thus *Bone Squash Diavolo* does not police black roguery in the end, but disperses it throughout the urban youth culture arising around it.

The conclusions in all these blackface plays free more agitated movement both on stage and beyond it in public style. Their farce makes zany the real tensions stressing American reality. No wonder this blackface theater grew simultaneously so popular and so feared. No wonder it called into being both an imperfect mixed public and strong opposition to that public's icons, songs, dances and, most of all, its totemic badge, the blackface mask. The argument over these contraries generated kinks in antebellum America that would not re-

lax, hopes that would not settle, and a blackened rogue whose entanglements became a convenient target for the struggle. A decade later,
agitated adaptation was still Rice's practice when he swapped out the
stately intonations Shakespeare had given Othello for New York black
and b'hoy rhythms representing ragged American character types in
Otello.

Blackness in this synthesis was new, but its antecedents included
European examples. Rather than promoting the usual European leg-
acy of arrested class, the rogue black also extended clues residual in
those earlier opponents of convention, Macheath and his gang in
John Gay's *The Beggar's Opera* (1728). When Ben Budge in that crew
claimed, "We are for a just part of the world, for every man hath a
right to enjoy life," the modern critic William Empson said: "Budge
anticipates Jefferson."[5] To which I add, Jefferson anticipates Jim Crow.
A century after Gay's ballad opera and a generation after Jefferson's
declaration, Jim Crow's continuing agitations emphasize, first, that
the enjoyment of life was a political issue for dark and poor people in
the States, and second, that John Gay, Thomas Jefferson, and Jim
Crow all pushed from their different directions toward completing
democracy.

Complementing his use of these fugitive black and white counter-
legacies, Jim Crow opposed theatrical support for patrimony and au-
tomatic entitlement. For both actors and audiences during the nineteenth century, Shakespeare's *Othello*, the play then most often staged
in North America, epitomized protection of authority. Shakespeare's
variant of the ancient Mediterranean fable about an outsider who
marries an eagerly disobedient daughter played in early America as
consolation. The stranger grew to realize the rude inadequacy of his
own culture and his resultant folly. Learning to agree with the convention that his revolt is inexcusable, the black outsider punished the
daughter and himself with death. A culture's love for dark intruders,

the plot of *Othello* seemed to report, was a problem that would eradicate itself. Jim Crow's allure challenged this consolation. Then Rice's *Otello* reversed it.

Unlike *Othello*, that previous model for thinking about race, Jim Crow is an intruder who does not resolve white nightmares with black self-erasure. Otello as played by the black rogue does not kill himself in self-disgust at the end. He survives with Desdemona to raise problems that go home with the audience. Most radically, this Otello and Desdemona live out the story's untold subtext. Their love produces interracial offspring, embodied on stage by Young Lorenzo Otello. The white woman and the black man not only kiss and promise to love their problem child; they enlist "the whole house" to further their pledge with celebratory dance and song. This is 1844, nearly two decades before Emancipation, a century before the word "racism" was coined, one hundred twenty-three years before the U.S. Supreme Court permitted interracial marriage in 1967.

As long as this conversion of reality lasts within the take-home meaning audiences recollect in tranquility, Jim Crow *fulfills* Jefferson. But he does so in the only way possible to ragged publics: by avoiding direct confrontation to come another day. He wheels awry, not away. Ralph Ellison called this behavior "running and dodging the forces of history rather than making a dominating stand." The dodginess of preterite ideas constitutes the major context of the Jim Crow plays. At once assertive and furtive, they churn up concepts conventionally unthinkable, then they slip away, surviving in the shadows to crop up again not quite traceably the same, in different guise, perhaps as rockabilly romanticism, or hip-hop aggression, or stand-up comedy in a political season.

Jim Crow's rude allure was not so much despite as *immanent in* a character's color and rags. Correctly understanding blacks as the most beleaguered segment of society, these plays and the public they orga-

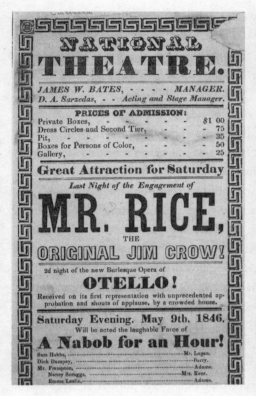

Figure 1. Otello *playbill, Cincinnati National Theatre, 9 May 1846. Note at List's end:* "Master Lorenzo Otello (eldest son of Otello and that there may be no partiality, nature has colored him half and half) . . . Master Kent." *Courtesy of the Harvard Theatre Collection, The Houghton Library.*

nized began marking runaway blacks as the group most symbolizing opposition to exclusion and disdain. To refuse this group was to emphasize the founding generation's compromised assertion of self-evident equality. Once this rogue blackness came in the house, however, it was able to rehearse ideas of itself pervasively and intensely. So intensely, indeed, that they came to enact what proved most elusive about the American compact—the promise of inclusion, of perfect union. This, then, has been the great paradox important in Jim Crow, that its name embodies both sides of the struggle to prompt or choke inclusion.

Certainly, the narrative of poor people marked black demanding their full franchise has dominated the popular culture that Americans have obsessively created at home since 1835 and exported since 1836, when T. D. Rice first played London, Paris, Dublin. The ideas Rice's plays scripted made their way indirectly, not against but behind the back of constitutional principles. They did not confront so much as assume and therefore mock the rhetoric of self-evidence. They registered the sort of democracy that the optimistically named United States was not achieving. Rice quite explicitly undercut belief in American agreement. He had Jim Crow refer in staged black English to "dis United State." He sang this coinage and he spelled it out in newspaper arguments with his critics.[6] In these ways, Jim Crow performance turned the minority experience of poor and young people in mixed areas along wharves and in many cities, North and South, into an imaginative construct that called out publics at large elsewhere to join the fray.

The afterlife of this construct is still doing similar work in late-night comedy, all the black musics from ragtime through hip-hop, fiction from *Native Son* to *Ragtime,* and in drama from *Porgy and Bess*—surely the American beggar's opera—to the two Lincoln plays of Suzan-Lori Parks. As a character, Jim Crow is Sambo's black sheep son, father to Uncle Tom, grandfather to Richard Wright's Native Son, metaphysical great-grandfather to Ellison's invisible youth. As a force, Jim Crow shares cultural DNA with both Ishmael Reed's Jes Grew (in *Mumbo Jumbo*) and Toni Morrison's "great class of undocumented men" (in *Tar Baby*). Of them all, Jim Crow is liveliest, cropping seasonally despite canonical opposition, his insistent momentum seeping among genres. It travels in no specific plot or casing but in its own fluid gesturation that gives heft to any performative mode. Jim Crow spreads wide because he is over-determined.

We can trace Jim Crow back to the gestures, then plays, that T. D. Rice brought into general acclaim, but doing so does not lead to celebration of authorial genius. It underlines, instead, the communion between a figure and a public that emerged together, demanding their due, stirring opposition that incited both their burial and their rebirth. Their teeming offspring reconvene successive generations. Their recrudescent icons become lightning rods for the integration necessary to resolve the evermore diagnostic American trauma. To see Jim Crow or any of his offspring is to converge with Americans of all sorts contesting what is real, what deserved, and to what length we will defer delivery of democracy. That is why the struggle over Jim Crow remains the central American issue.

Notes

1. Juretta Hecksher, "'Our National Poetry': The Afro-Chesapeake Inventions of African American Dance," in *Ballroom, Boogie, Shimmy Sham, Shake: A Social and Popular Dance Reader,* ed. Julie Malnig (Urbana: University of Illinois Press, 2009), pp. 19–35.

2. For John Crow, see John F. Szwed and Roger D. Abrahams, "After the Myth: Studying Afro-American Cultural Patterns in the Plantation Literature," *Research in African Literatures* 7, no. 2 (Fall 1976): 125–126, 299. For a story about a slaver-Chief doomed to eternity as a Buzzard, see Edward C. L. Adams, *Tales of the Congaree,* with an introduction by Robert G. O'Meally; reprint, 1927 (Chapel Hill: University of North Carolina Press, 1987), pp. 120–121.

3. Ishmael Reed, *Mumbo Jumbo,* reprint, 1972 (New York: Atheneum, 1988), p. 162.

4. Bessie Jones and Bess Lomax Hawes, *Step It Down: Games, Plays, Songs, and Stories from the African-American Heritage* (New York: Harper and Row, 1972), p. 55.

5. Empson is discussing *The Beggar's Opera*, 2.1.19–20: William Empson, *Some Versions of Pastoral* (London: Chatto and Windus, 1950), p. 220.

6. W. T. Lhamon, Jr., *Jump Jim Crow: Plays, Lyrics, and Street Prose of the First Atlantic Popular Culture* (Cambridge, Mass.: Harvard University Press, 2003), p. 23.

Note on the Text

These scripts are the smoking guns of America's racial formation. Wheeling and dodging in these acts, whiteness and blackness meet to blast themselves into being. These early performances about Jim Crow impersonate blacks, but not as the despised or frightening antagonists we might expect whites to create deep in the slavery era. This early Jim Crow is instead an agent acting out for his low, mostly white, audience the resentments they feel. His dissatisfactions are theirs, but *more so*, symbolically intensified, because his blackface makeup signals that he is even more oppressed than they. His tight spots rehearse their worst-case scenario. His quick quips and improvised rhymes spinning away from trouble project their own fantasied survival strategies.

Like other originary scenes discovered late in a created life, these plays now profoundly surprise their offspring—you and me. Far more complex than their reputation, these acts oppose both racism and slavery. They also celebrate their idea of blackness as desirable behavior in an early Republic that was failing its multitudes.

Jim Crow, American provides two plays that a young white actor named Thomas Dartmouth Rice wrote to extend his early success all across the country, New Orleans to New York. It adds *Otello*, Rice's stunning alteration of the *Othello* plot. This final play culminates his meditation on street language, cross-racial attraction, and cultural integration. Together, these plays show that Rice's work makes a radioactive template for thinking about race meshing with class in Atlantic life. (Interested readers will find more of Rice's plays, including those that others wrote for him to perform in England—with supporting songs, informal street prose, and a capacious account—in my earlier anthology, *Jump Jim Crow* [2002].)

Think of the three American scripts given here as the inventive homework an actor and his low public performed together. This public was chiefly white but included blacks, both North and South. Together, though unevenly, they established an American black rogue as the charismatic token of all the multitudes not franchised politically or economically—not then and not yet. The politics that quashed them in spite of their cultural centrality yielded unintended consequences that keep on giving.

Every time a youth culture in America feels its beans, it reconstitutes itself around versions of Jim Crow. Thus Jim Crow begat most of Harriet Beecher Stowe's black characters (her novel is inconceivable without Rice's extravaganzas), the ragtime Bert Williams, and the Jazz Era Porgy. Those progeny begat, in turn, Al Jolson going to heaven on a mule (*Wonder Bar*, 1934) and Fred Astaire channeling Bojangles in blackface (*Swing Time*, 1936). Elvis in the 1950s and Eminem at the end of the century had all the gestures by which we recognize family resemblance; they were doing Jim Crow un-masked.

This continuing return of the repressed ensures that Rice's foundational plays remain the quintessential texts of American culture. They register, define, and integrate the unresolved American traumas of race and class.

Chronology

The Jim Crow figure blends European lumpen humor with African American folklore. On the European side, its clear antecedents are a strain of Atlantic theater fascinated with lowlife behaving badly: cozening scammers, Pistol, Falstaff, and Shakespeare's conventional fools, Richard Brome's *The Jovial Crew*, Daniel Defoe's reportage, and the Tom and Jerry comedies on the London stage in the early nineteenth century. From this side of the Atlantic came the dance steps and mocking cackle that Rice learned observing black cutting contests at New York's Catharine Market as a boy. He would have supplemented these with gestural moves and songs he observed on what was then the Southwestern frontier, Mobile to Louisville, Pittsburgh to New Orleans. John Gay's Macheath (1728) and Douglas Jerrold's Beau Nash (1834) echo in Rice's character Bone Squash. But Bone is also a figure of American "blackness," as whites appropriated and reimagined it to codify their own disaffections.

That's the way things stood through the 1830s, when the American codification of this cultural process intensified. By the 1840s, Jim Crow had spawned offspring that would live their own lives. Ned Christy was performing black songs in Buffalo as early as 1837; he soon formed the Christy Minstrels. In the winter of 1842–1843, Dan Emmett's Virginia Minstrels would take the stage in lower Manhattan. These blackface rogues were absorbing and compressing more meaning, including the racist ridicule that is now the conventional understanding of American blackface minstrelsy. Although some accomplished black professionals were working this mode from the 1830s on—Old Cornmeal in New Orleans, William Henry Lane ("Master Juba") in New York, then England—the white phenomenon dominated. After the Civil War and Emancipation, however, black troupes began holding their own against the white companies, all of them wearing black makeup through the second decade of the twentieth century, and often later. Appearing in theaters, wherever they could, and tent shows, sometimes they accompanied circuses; sometimes they pared down to accompany hucksters and medicine shows. Always they combined singing, dancing, and comedy. Race relations were their constant topic, in all their modes. Their skits evolved gradually into confrontations between a fancy-talking interlocutor, who impersonated white pretense, and so-called end men, who impersonated black raggedness, syncopating rhythms with their tambourine and bones. The end men scoffed at the interlocutor's attempts to maintain discipline. They made an art of talking back under cover of playing stupid—Bert Williams's acts in vaudeville and early twentieth-century theater are a good example. Their shenanigans documented what was possible on a deeply skewed playing field. As a rule, these companies attracted both black and white audiences, often together for the same shows, but also generally segregated by section.

Both the white and the black traveling shows fell away rapidly at the onset of the Civil Rights insurgences of the late 1950s, yet amateur performances persisted for another quarter-century, even as reformist groups worked to ban them. By then, however, the coded gestures of blackface were thoroughly dispersed into other modes—so much so that indeed much of vaudeville, nearly all of ragtime, a lot of jazz and early Hollywood, and nearly all of rock 'n' roll, rap, and hip-hop have been blackface in all but makeup.

JIM CROW, AMERICAN

SONGS

Before there were Jim Crow plays, there was "Jump Jim Crow," first as a folk song and dance, then gradually as an improvised stage performance that became its own extravaganza. T. D. Rice would sing and dance the song, then pretend to try to stop; his audience would demand multiple encores. This song was unstable in every way. Its few core verses continually changed as they adapted to the performance contexts. They never, for instance, decided if Jim Crow's birth was in Kentucky or Virginia. The chorus was always fully half the song and embodied the need to leap out of itself. And rather than providing an authoritative text, the printed versions increased the song's flux by modeling its improvisation.

The Original Jim Crow[1]

1

Come listen all you galls and boys
I's jist from Tuckyhoe,[2]
I'm goin to sing a little song,
My name is Jim Crow
   Chorus:
     Weel about and turn about and do jis so,
     Eb'ry time I weel about and jump Jim Crow.

2

Oh I'm a roarer on de Fiddle,
And down in old Virginny,
They say I play de skyentific
Like Massa Pagannini.[3]

3

I git 'pon a flat boat
I cotch de Uncle Sam,
Den I went to see de place
Where dey kill'd Packenham.[4]

4

I went down to de riber,
I did'nt mean to stay,
But dere I see so many galls,
I could'nt get away.

5

An den I go to Orleans
An feel so full of fight
Dey put me in de Calaboose,
An keep me dare all night.

6

When I got out I hit a man,
His name I now forgot,
But dere was nothing left
'Sept a little grease spot.

7

I wip my weight in wildcats
I eat an Alligator,
And tear up more ground
Dan kifer 50 load of tater.

8

I sit upon a Hornet's nest,
I dance upon my head,
I tie a Wiper[5] round my neck
And den I goes to bed.

9

Dere's Possum up de gumtree
An Raccoon in de hollow,
Wake Snakes for June bugs
Stole my half a dollar.

10

A ring tail'd monkey
An a rib nose Babboon,
Went out de odder day
To spend de arternoon.

11

Oh de way dey bake de hoecake[6]
In old Virginny neber tire
Dey put de doe upon de foot
An hole it to de fire.

12

Oh by trade I am a carpenter,
But be it understood,
De way I get my liben is,
By sawing de tick oh wood.

13

I'm a full blooded niggar,
Ob de real ole stock,
An wid my head and shoulder
I can split a horse block.

14

I struck a Jarsey niggar,
In de street de oder day,
An I hope I neber stir
If he didn't turn gray.

15

I'm berry much afraid of late
Dis jumping will be no good.
For while de Crow are dancing,
De Wites will saw de wood.

16

But if dey get honest,
By sawing wood like slaves
Der'es an end to de business,
Ob our friend Massa Hays.[7]

17

I met a Philadelphia niggar
Dress'd up quite nice & clean
But de way he 'bused de Yorkers
I thought was berry mean.

18

So I knocked down dis Sambo
And shut up his light,
For I'm jist about as sassy,
As if I was half white.

19

But he soon jumped up again,
An 'gan for me to feel,
Says I go away you niggar,
Or I'll skin you like an eel.

20

I'm so glad dat I'm a niggar,
An dont you wish you was too
For den you'd gain popularity
By jumping Jim Crow.

21

Now my brodder niggars,
I do not think it right,
Dat you should laugh at dem
Who happen to be white.

22

Kase it dar misfortune,
And dey'd spend ebery dollar,
If dey only could be
Gentlemen ob colour.

23

It almost break my heart,
To see dem envy me,
An from my soul I wish dem,
Full as black as we.

24

What stuf it is in dem,
To make de Debbil black
I'll prove dat he is white
In de twinkling of a crack.

25

For you see loved brodders,
As true as he hab a tail,
It is his berry wickedness,
What makes him turn pale.

26

I went to Hoboken,
To hab a promenade,
An dar I see de pretty gals,
Drinking de Lemonade.

27

Dat sour and dat sweet,
Is berry good by gum',
But de best of lemonade is,
Made by adding rum.

28

At de Swan cottage,
Is de place I tink,
Whar dey make dis'licious,
An 'toxicating drink.

29

Some go to Weehawk,
An some to Brooklyn hight
But dey better stay at home,
If dey want to see de sight.

30

To go to de museum,
I'm sure it is dare duty,
If for noting else,
Jist to see de sleeping beauty.

31

An dare is daddy Lambert,[8]
An a skeleton on he hunkie,
An likeness of Broadway dandy
In a glass case of monkies.

32

De Broadway bells,
When dey carry full sail,
Around dem wear a funny ting,
Just like a fox tail.

33

When you hear de name of it,
I sure it make you roar,
Why I ax'd 'em what it was,
And dey said it was a boar.

34

De great Nullification,
And fuss in de South,
Is now before Congress,
To be tried by word ob mouth.

35

Dey hab had no blows yet,
And I hope dey nebber will,
For its berry cruel in bredren,
One anoders blood to spill.

36

Wid Jackson at de head,
Dey soon de ting may settle
For ole Hickory is a man,
Dat's tarnal full ob mettle.

37

Should dey get to fighting,
Perhaps de blacks will rise,
For deir wish for freedom,
Is shining in deir eyes.

38

An if de blacks should get free,
I guess dey'll fee some bigger,
An I shall concider it,
A bold stroke for de niggar.

39

I'm for freedom,
An for Union altogether,
Aldough I'm a black man,
De white is call'd my broder.

40

I'm for union to a gal,
An dis is a stubborn fact,
But if I marry an dont like it,
I'll nullify de act.

41

I'm tired of being a single man
An I'm tarmined to get a wife
For what I think de happiest
Is de swee married life.

42

Its berry common 'mong de white
To marry and get divorced
But dat I'll nebber do
Unless I'm really forced.

43

I think I see myself in Broadway
Wid my wife upon my arm,
And to follow up de fashion,
Dere sure can be no harm.

44

An I caution all white dandies,
Not to come in my way,
For if dey insult me,
dey'll in de gutter lay.

Jim Crow, Still Alive!!!⁹

1

De way to bake a hoe cake
Ol Virginny nebber tire,
Stick de hoe cake on de foot,
And hold it to de fire.
So I wheel about
I turn about
I do just so,
And ebry time I wheel about
I jump Jim Crow.

2

Old Sam Peacock
Stole a side of leather

Well done Sam
Cant you go and steal anoder
So I wheel, etc.

3
Dere's meat upon de goosefoot,
And marrow on de bone,
Dere's pretty gals at our house,
An mamma's not at home.
So I wheel, etc.

4
I listed in de army
An sarve Uncle Sam,
Any other service
Aint worth a damn.
So I wheel, etc.

5
At New Orleans town
De British went to teal,
But when dey see ol Hickory,
Day took to dere heel.
So I wheel, etc.

6
Lord how dey cut dirt,
An didn't stop to trifle.
For dey didn't like de sight
Ob de dam Yankee rifle.
So I wheel, etc.

7
I'm a touch of the snapping turtle,
Nine-tenths of a bull dog.

I've turned the Mississippy,
All for a pint of grog.
So I wheel, etc.

8

I went to New York,
And I tink I cut a swell,
And de first place I stopp'd at,
Was Holt's new Hotel.[10]
So I wheel, etc.

9

I went up stairs
To peep at de nation,
And dere I met Ol Hays[11]
An all de Corporation.[12]
So I wheel, etc.

10

An Alderman got up to top,
And called for a glass ob gin,
Says he, I'm nearer Heaven
Dan I shall ever be agin.
So I wheel, etc.

11

Dey had so many good tings
As true as I'm a sinner,
I tink rader went a head
Ob de Corporation dinner.
So I wheel, etc.

12

Dey bid me help myself
An cut and come again,

An sure I wasnt slow
When dey brought de Campaigne[13]
So I wheel, etc.

13

But I dont admire de liquor,
It berry good for some,
But we gentleman of color,
Always prefer de niggar rum.

14

When I was in Philadelphia,
I had to laugh in de treet,
To see de butcher women
In de market selling meat.

15

Dere you can see women
Slipping on like a sled,
With a tub full of mackarel
Which dey carry on de head.

16

Sister Dinah hab gib a hint.
Dat Avery will swing[14]
An on dat gran occasion,
A verse or two I'll sing.

17

It is his last appearance
I guess upon de stage,
An I tink de naughty feller
Will exit in a rage.

18

Now my verses are de best kind,
And dis I'm sure's no bore,
For ebry time I dance and sing,
De people cry encore.

19

For poets are a poor set,
As you must all know,
For de more dey try to write,
De poorer dey do grow.
So I wheel, etc.

20

Oh I saw a dandy niggar wench,
An I thought dat I should die,
When I saw her wink at me,
An roll round her eye.

21

She was brack as de debbil,
An she hab such a squint,
Dat when she wink at me
I couldn't take he hint.

22

Election's coming on,
An I'll try if I can,
Just be elected for a 'Sembly man.

23

I tink if I get in,
I should suit em to a hair,

An de next ting dey would do
Would be to make me mayor.

24

For de duties ob de Semblyman
I tink is very funny,
For dey only hab to eat dinners,
And spend de people's money.

25

Dey dont mind what folks say,
Tho' it comes from every quarter,
An all de people wants
Is a little wholesome water.[15]

26

But dat don consarn dem,
For what do you tink!
Why water is de only ting
Dat dey do not drink.

27

I stopt at Washington City,
The capital ob de nation,
An I ax'd Massa Jackson
To gib me situation.

28

Says he, Jim Crow,
What can you do?
I can nullify de boot,
An put de veto on de shoe.

29

Says he, Jim Crow,
What can you do for me?
Says I, Massa Jackson,
I can plant a hickory tree.

30

Forty-eleben debbils
Lived in Noah's ark,
Jona was de fisherman
What swallowed down de shark.

31

It rained forty days,
An it rained forty nites,
And Noah's Ark rested
On de Brooklyn Hites.

32

Oh by trade I am a carpenter
But be it understood,
De way I get a liben is
By sawing de stick ob wood.

33

I hab a sneaking notion,
If dere's fun to be had,
Its not in skinning cat-fish,
Or in eating raw shad.

34

I was at a ball de oder night,
A lady tried to faint,

We poured water on her face,
Not tinking der was paint.

35
And sich a nasty figgur,
I'm sure was neber seen,
A face wid streaks of red and white,
Dat before looked berry clean.

36
Dis song is getting long
But will be longer still,
For I am full 'tarmined
To give you your fill.

37
If you want to buy a song,
De one you like you'll meet,
At five hundred seventy two
North Second Street[16]

38
If I were a regular sweep,
I'd set the town a ringing,
So musical my verses are,
For scantimental singing.

39
But de real fun of all is,
And dis you all well know,
Is to gib de scientific touch,
Ob jumping Jim Crow.
So I wheel, etc.

40

I'm a full blooded niggar,
Ob de real old stock,
An wid my head and shoulders
I can split a horse block.

41

I struck a Jarsey niggar,
In de street de oder day,
An I hope I neber stir,
If he did'nt turn grey.

42

I'm berry much afraid ob late,
Dis jumping will be no good,
For while de Crows are dancing,
De *Whites* will saw de wood.

43

But if dey get honest,
By sawing wood like slaves,
Dere's an end to the business
Ob our friend Massa Hays.

44

I met a New York niggar,
Dress'd up quite clean,
But de way he bused de Delphians,
I thought was bery mean.

45

So I knock'd down dis Sambo
And shut up his light,

For I'm jist about as sassy,
As if I was half white.

46
But he soon jumped up again,
An 'gan for me to feel,
Says I, go away you niggar,
Or I'll skin you like an eel.

47
Dere's anoder niggar,
As cunning as a fox.
He's a great steam scourer,
And his name is dandy Cox.

48
I hab a gal in dis city,
She's as quick as a trigger,
And she neber look so handsome,
As when kiss'd by a niggar.

49
A white kiss is good enouff
But it don't sound so keen,
As when given by a brack man,
Wid a great broad grin.

50
When I do kiss the lubly creatures,
I screw my mouth just so,
For it makes me feel so bery good,
Dat I don't know what to do.

51

But I neber kissed a white gal,
And I hope I nebber will;
For you hab to be so delicate,
You cannot get your fill.

52

I went to de chicken coop
An got upon my knees,
I tink I die a laughing
To hear de chickens sneeze.

53

De great Nullification,
And de fuss in the South,
Is now before Congress
To be tried by de word ob mouth.

54

Dey hab had no blows yet,
An I hope dey nebber will,
For it's berry cruel in bredren,
One anoder's blood to spill.

55

Wid Jackson at de head
Dey soon dis ting may settle
For ol Hickory is a man
Dat's tarnal full ob mettle.

56

Should dey go to fighting,
Perhaps de bracks will rise,

For der wish for freedom
Is shining in der eyes.

57

An if de bracks should get free,
I guess dey'll feel som bigger,
I shall consider it
A bo'd stroke for de niggar.

58

I am for freedom
An for union altogeder,
Although I am a brack man,
De white is called my broder.

59

What stuff it is in dem,
To make de debbil brack,
I'll prove dat he is white,
In de twinkling of a crack.
So I wheel about, etc.

60

For you see loved brodders,
As true as he hab a tail,
It is his berry wickedness,
What makes he turn pale.

61

I went to de Camden,
To hab a promenade.
And dare I saw de dretty gals,
Drinking de lemonade.

62

Dat sour and dat sweet,
Is berry good by gum,
But de best of lemonade is
Made by adding rum.

63

At de Swan cottage,
Is de place I tink,
Whar dey make dis liscious
And toxicating drink.

64

De Filedelfia grog shop,
You can see as dey pass,
And dey sell de best ob lekier
For three cents a glass.

65

Some go to Weehawk
And some to Brooklyn heights
But dey better stay at home
If dey want to see de sights.

66

To go to de museum
I'm sure it is der duty
If for notting else
Just to see de sleeping beauty.

67

And dere is Daddy Lambert[17]
An a skeleton on he hunkies.

And likeness of Broadway dandy,
In a glass case of monkies.

68

Dere was one Sam Patch[18]
Who took de ugly leap,
He'd better stay in York,
And be a chimney sweep.

69

An if he minded he profession
An not to fond of de cup
When oders was getting down
He'd sure be getting up.

70

I seen a pretty gal,
Wid a tipet and a muff,
I don't know what her trade is,
But I guess she's up to snuff.

71

She went in de dry goods store,
An winked at de clerk,
She ax'd him to come to her house,
A little arter dark.

72

He went to de three bells,
He watch went up de spout,
Kase de master was in de store,
An he no chance for sourkrout.

73

Dis wicked boy do dat,
All for a painted face,
Which berry soon I see
Will bring him to disgrace.

74

I'm for union to a gal
An dis is a stubborn fact,
Dat if I marry an don't like it,
I'll nullify de act.

75

I'm sure dere be gals enuff,
To hab a fair chance,
An if I don't get a good un,
I'll laugh it off an dance.

76

I'm tired ob being a single man,
An I'm tarmin'd to git a wife,
For what I tink de happiest,
Is de sweet married life.

77

Its berry common 'mong de whites
To marry and git divorc'd,
But dat I'll deber do,
Unless I'm really forced.

78

I tink I see myself on Rail Road,
Wid a wife upon my arm,

An to foller up de fashun,
Dare sure can be no harm.

79

An I caution all de white dandies
Not to come in my way,
For as sure as they insult me,
Dey'll in de gutter lay.

80

De Chesnut street belles,
When dey carry full sail
Around dem wear a funny ting,
Just like a fox' tail.

81

When you har de name of it,
I sure it make you roar.
Why I ax'd em what it was,
And dey said it was a bore.

82

My sister dinah I see
Has made a great debut
But she cannot dance like me
No more den one ob you.

83

She's my sista it is true,
But dat is not de ting,
For what is de use ob wenches
Trying to jump play and sing.

84

Dare's sista Cuffelena,
Now she hab more sense,
Dan to fool away her time,
An at her own expense.

85

And Cuffelena hab got a plan,
Into effect she'll carry.
And dat is to make a match,
And her lubly Sambo marry.

86

But as for poor Dinah,
Its just as mudder said,
She be a bery sassy gal,
Wid a soft piece on de head.

87

She's a tarnal sassy niggar,
As you I guess can see,
Or she would'nt make a fuss,
And try to blaguard me.

88

Now my brodder niggars,
I do not tink it right,
Dat you should laugh at dem,
Who happen to be white.

89

Kase its dar misfortune,
An dey'd spend every dollar

If dey could only be
Gentlemen ob colour.

90

It almost break my heart,
To see dem envy me,
And from my soul I wish dem
Full as brack as we.

91

For I am as true a nigger
As ever yet was born,
An I am little fractious
When I hab a small horn.[19]

92

For I'm of a dancing family,
An I'd radder dance dan pray,
For ob de two professions,
De dancing's de best pay.

93

As I was born in a cane break,
An Dinah in a dough-trough,
I hope you'll see de difference,
And hussle her off.

94

Now before I leave you,
One ting I hab to ask,
If de making ob dese verses
Be not a plagy task.

95

But if you're not contented,
An tink it is not right,
I'll come agen some oder time,
An dance all night.

96

Now white folks, white folks,
Don't take offence,
An when I take a benefit,
I'll treat to stone fence.[20]

97

Farewell, farewell,
But dont cry encore,
You now had 100 verses,
Nex time I gib you more.

98

O white folks, white folks,
I glad to hear you holler,
But I'll not jump Jim Crow 'gin
Unless you hit me wid a dollar.

De Original Jim Crow[21]

Oh Jim Crow's cum again, as you must all know
For he wheel about, he jump about, he do just so,
  And ebery time he jump about, he jump Jim Crow.
  So I wheel about, I turn about,
  I do just so,
  And ebery time I wheel about,

I jump Jim Crow.
I kneel to de buzzard, and I bow to de crow,
An ebery time I wheel about, I jump Jim Crow,
> So I wheel about, &c.
I stopt at Washington City, as I came from de West,
An went for to see de great President.
> So I wheel about, &c.
I meet ole Andy at de corner ob de street,
Says he, Jim Crow, an't you gwan for to treat.
> So I wheel about, &c.
So I pull'd out my pocket-book, I didn't mind expense
An went in an got a horn ob good stone fence.[22]
> So I wheel about, &c.
An arter I had treated him to a smaller ob de best
I went to count my money, an found but a quarter left.
> So I wheel about, &c.
Den, says he, Jim Crow, I know what are at,
You cum for an office, an I'll make you my shoe black
> So I wheel about, &c.
De Kentucky niggas dey libs on mush,
But de Philadelphia niggas, dey say "Oh, Hush!"
> So I wheel about, &c.
De New York niggas, dey tink dey are free,
Case dey all out ob de penitentiary.
> So I wheel about, &c.
De New York loafers dey cum here to teal
Dey cum up de market and tole a leg ob veal.
> So I wheel about, &c.
Old folks, old folks you'd better go to bed,
Case you only put de debil in de young folks hed.
> So I wheel about, &c.

A ring tail'd monkey and a ribb'd nose baboon,
Went out de oder day to spend de arternoon.
  So I wheel about, &c.
So den at night dey went to drink dere tea,
De one drank Shoushong, de oder bohea.
  So I wheel about, &c.
I met Miss Dinah, an I gin her a buss,
She slapt me in de face and made a mighty fuss.
  So I wheel about, &c.
Snake bak'd a hoe cake, and set de frog to watch it,
De frog fell asleep, and de lizard come an cotch'd it.
  So I wheel about, &c.
I cum to a riber an couldn't get across,
So I gib half a dolla for an old blind horse.
  So I wheel about, &c.
I druv this horse up a hill, an just as he got to de top
He fell down and got kill'd, an den I couldn't swop.
  So I wheel about, &c.
Dere's Van Buren, he's firmly bent,
To hold himself up for de next President.[23]
  So I wheel about, &c.
Now if I was President ob dese United States,
I'd drink mint julep, an swing upon de gates.
  So I wheel about, &c.
Oh, massa gib me holiday I staid ober time,
So he hung me up and gib me sweet thirty nine.
  So I wheel about, &c.
Oh, Jim Crow struck a man, his name I forgot,
But dare was notin left but a little grease spot.
  So I wheel about, &c.
I'm for union to a gal, an dis is a stubborn fact,

But if I marry an don't like it, I'll nullify de act.
  So I wheel about, &c.
I'm tired ob being single, so I'm tarmined to git a wife,
[F]or what I tink de happiest, is de sweet married life.
  So I wheel about, &c.
I tink I see myself in Broadway, wid wife upon my arm,
An to follow up de fashion, dere sure can be no harm.
  So I wheel about, &c.
Oh, white folks, white folks, I see your up to snuff,
I'm berry much afraid dat you neber get enuff.
  So I wheel about, &c.

Jim Crow[24]

OLD JIM CROW's come agin, as you must all know,
And ebery body say I cum to jump Jim Crow
  Chorus.—Weel about and turn about, and do jis so.
      Ebery time I weel about, I jump Jim Crow.

My name is Daddy Rice, as you berry well do know,
And none in de Nited States like me, can jump Jim Crow.

I was born in a cane break, and cradled in a trough,
Swam de Mississippi, whar I cotch'd de hoopen coff.

To whip my weight in wild cats, eat an alligator,
And drink de Mississippi dry, I'm de very *critter.*

I went to de woods, heard a debil of a howl,
I look'd up a tree, and saw a great owl.

I off wid my hat, stuck my heel in de ground,
And then went to work to grin the owl down.

I grinn'd wid my eyes open, and den wid um shut,
But I could not diskiver dat I stirred de owl a foot.

Den I grinn'd slantendicular, den wid one eye,
'Twould have done your soul good to see de feathers fly.

Den I climb'd up de tree, and I wish I may be shot,
If I had'nt been grinning at a great pine knot.

I'm like de frost in ole December, git my foot widin de ground,
Takes a hook and ladder company to try to pull me down.

And eben when you get me down, I melt and run about,
You'll hab to send for engine, to cum and put me out.

Though you tink you got me out, some heat dar will remain,
Nex morning, bright and early, I'll be blazing up agin.

I've been to old Kentucky, whar I hab you for to know,
Dat all de pretty ladies dar lub Jim Crow.

I've been to Philadelphia, New York and Baltimore,
But when I got to Boston, it beat all I'd seen before.

Dey build most all dar houses out ob brick and stone,
Dey run em up so high, dey almost reach de moon.

Dey talk ob de Philadelphia markets, an de New York markets,
    loud,
But de ole market, here in Boston, will be seen among de crowd.

No matter what is wantin, in de market you can buy
From a quarter of an ox, down to a punkin pie.

Dare is someting I gwaing to tell you, which I want you all to
    know,
Dare is a pretty lady here, in lub wid Jim Crow.

Lor bless de lubly creature, I teach dem how to dance,
And show dem de new step, just arrived from France.

Dis is de style of Alabama, what dey hab in Mobile,
And dis is Louisiana, whar dey trike upon de heel.

Here's Virginny double trouble, whar dey dance de corn chuck,
And dere's de real scientific, what dey hab in Kentuck.

Here's de long Island ube,[25] or de hunck ober dee,
And here's de Georgia step, by de double rule ob tree.

Here's de kneel to Carleton's daughter, what dey hab in Indian,
And here's de old Mississippi step, and fetch it if you can.

And dare is ole Virginny, she cut a pretty figger,
I neber go dar, kase dey don't respect de nigger.

It was twelve o'clock de udder night, or somewhere dare about,
I took my finger for de snuffers, and put de candle out.

De debil take de noise when de nigger is so tire.
When along came watchman, and hollar, fire!! fire!!

O, I got out ob de bed, put on my close widout much fright,
And started for de fire, in de middle ob de night.

When I got to de fire, I did'nt know what to do.
But I heard a gemman cry, lay hold ob No. 2.

I went up to de Colonel, and ax'd how he'd ben,
He say, you sassy nigger, you lay hold ob No. 10.

I work hard at de engine, den de foreman send for rum,
Jolly, how my eye glisten, wen I see it cum.

When I saw de eatables a comin, says I, if you please,
I'll thank you for a stiffer, and hunk ob bread and cheese.

I take one horn, and den I take anoder,
When I drink more, white man call me brudder.

Den I went down to Ann Street, did'nt mean to stay,
But dey took me to de watch house, and I couldn't get away.

And de tin pot alley, de niggers had a hop,
I went in a little while, didn't mean to stop.

The house was topsy turvy, all turned upside down,
And de niggers had de dance ten foot under groun.

De wite folks get a barrel of flour, and knock'd de head in,
And den de way dey cried fire, I'm sure it was a sin.

De niggers rushed out, as if it was a shower,
And when dey got up stair, dey let'em hab de flour.

And such a set ob niggers, I'm sure was neber seen,
And such fun in white folk, I tink was berry mean.

I was liv'd in ole Virginny, and dey used to gib me
Hoe cakes, sassafras, and shangalanga tea.

De way dey bake de hoe cake, in old Virginny neber tire,
Dey put de cake upon de foot, and hold de foot to de fire.

If nature make me black man, and oder folks white,
I went to ole Boston, where dey learn me left and right.

I went into de cradle, where dey rock'd sweet Liberty,
And dare I saw de names ob those who made their country free.

I went across to Charlestown, and on to Bunker Hill,
Which once de British tried to climb, but found it diffikil.

'Twas dare I saw de Navy Yard, likewide de Dry Dock.
'Twas lin'd by de best ob stone, dug out ob Quincy Rock.

Near it lay de ship ob war, among dem de Constitution,
Which our brave heroes sail'd in, and put England in
    confusion.

De finest fun dat ever happened, was in de city ob New York,
When dey told de British soger it was time to walk and talk.

Dey did'nt know what to tink ob it, when dey found dey must
    be gone,
Kase dey hab no shoe or tocking on, and cold wedder comin
    on.

So dey gaddered up dare fixeds, and 'gan to march away,
And sailed for land ob Johnny Bull, about de brake ob day.

When dey got back to England dey didn't fear de debbil,
Buy dey radder be excused, dan fight wid Yankee rebel.

For dey are like a piece ob India rubber, you may hit 'em on de
    sconce,
De harder dat you knock 'em down, de higher up they bounce.

Dare's a place dey call de Boson, once fought for liberty,
Dey'd throw de nullifiers overboard, as once dey did de tea.

Dar's two ole sogers, whose names me no forget,
One was massa George Washington, de oder Laughayit.

When de war was ober, and ebery ting content,
De people make George Washington de great President.

Den he put all de States togedder, and tied a string around,
And when de string is broken, boys, dey'll tumble to de ground.

When dey was first set up, dare was only a dozen and one,
But now dare is twenty-four, and a number more to cum.

Dese twenty-four children belong to Uncle Sam,
And hab been bery dutiful, except now and den.

You all know who Uncle Sam is, from de captain to de mate,
He's de fader of de children ob dese Nited State.

He's got a handsome fortune by industry's made,
And now his chief concern is, to gib his children a trade.

He's got one sassy daughter, her name is Caroline,
I'm 'fraid he'll hab to tie her up and gib her 39.

Now as for South Carlina, she'd better keep her passion in,
Or else she'll get a licken now, before she does begin.

Johnny C. Calhoun is courting her, dey say he's got de wedding
    ring,
And when de weddin' ober, dey are going to make him king.

When he walks up to Caroline, her sun-bright hand to take,
Be careful de wedding ring don't turn out to be an Irish wake.

Dey say South Carolina is a fool, and as for Johnny C. Calhoun,
He'll be worse dan Davy Crockett, when he tried to fool de
    coon.

Oh, he took up his crooked gun, and fired round de maple tree,
De ball came back in de same place, and hit him on de knee.

O, wite folks, wite folks, I see you up to snuff,
I'm bery much afraid dat you neber get anuff.

Now wite folks, wite folks, please to let me go.
And I'll cum back anuder night and jump Jim Crow.

Clare de Kitchen[26]

In old Kentuck in de arter noon,
We sweep de floor wid a bran new broom,
And arter dat we form a ring,
And dis de song dat we do sing,
    Oh! Clare de kitchen old folks, young folks,
    Clare de kitchen old folks young folks,
    Old Virginny never tire.

2

I went to de creek, I cou'dn't get a cross,
I'd nobody wid me but an old blind horse;
But old Jim Crow came riding by,
Says he, old fellow your horse will die.
    Its Clare de kitchen &c.

3

My horse fell down upon de spot,
Says he "don't you see his eyes is sot";
So I took out my knife and off wid his skin,
And when he comes to life I'll ride him agin.
    So Clare de kitchen &c.

4

A jay-bird sot on a hickory limb,
He wink'd at me and I wink'd at him;
I picked up a stone and I hit his shin,
Says he you better not do dat agin.
    He Clar'd de kitchen &c.

5

A Bull-frog dress'd in sogers close,[27]
Went in a field to shoot some crows;
De crows smell powder and fly away,
De Bull-frog mighty mad dat day.
    So Clare de kitchen &c.

6

Den I went down wid Cato Moore,
To see de Steam-boat come ashore;
Ev'ry man for himself, so I pick'd up a trunk—
Leff off, said the Captain, or I burn you wid a chunk.
    And Clare de kitchen &c.

7

I hab a sweetheart in dis town,
She wears a yellow striped gown;
And when she walks de streets around,
De hollow of her foot makes a hole in de ground.[28]
    Now Clare de kitchen &c.

8

Dis love is a ticklish ting you know,
It makes abody feel all over so;
I put de question to Coal black Rose,
She's as black as ten of spades, and got a lubly flat nose
    So Clare de kitchen &c.

9

Go away says she, wid your cowcumber[29] shin,
If you come here agin I stick you wid a pin;
So I turn on my heel and I bid her good bye,

And arter I was gone, she began for to cry.
    Oh! Clare de kitchen &c.

10

So now I'se up and off you see,
To take a julep sangaree;
I'll sit upon a tater hill,
And eat a little Whip-poor-will.
    So Clare de kitchen &c.

11

I wish I was back in old Kentuck,
For since I left it I had no luck;
De galls so proud dey won't eat mush,
And when you go to court'em dey say O hush.
    Its Clare de kitchen &c.

Gombo Chaff [30]

On de Ohio bluff in de state of Indiana,
Dere's where I live, chock up to de Habbanna.
Eb'ry mornin early Massa gib me licker,
I take my net and paddle and I put out de quicker,
I jump into my kiff. And I down de river driff,
And I cotch as many cat fish as ever nigger liff.

2

Now dis morning on a driff-log tink I see an Alligator,
I scull my skiff around and chuck him sweet potato,
I cratch him on de head and try for to vex it,
But I could'nt fool de varmint no how I could fix it;

So I picks up a brick an' I fotch'd him sich a lick,
But twant nothin' but a pine knot 'pon a big stick.

3

Now old Massa build a barn to put de fodder in,
Dis ting an dat ting an' one ting anodder;
Thirty ninth Decembur time come a rise ob water,
An' it carry Massa barn much farder dan it ought to;
Then old Massa swear he cuss an' tare his hair,
Becase de water tuck barn off he couldn't tell where.

4

Now old Massa die on de 'lebenteenth of April,
I put him in de troff what cotch de sugar maple,
I digs a deep hole right out upon de level,
An' I do believe sure enough he's gone to de debil,
For when he live you know he light upon me so,
But now he's gone to tote de firewood way down below.

5

Den Missis she did marry Big Bill de weaver,
Soon she found out he was a gay deceiver,
He grab all de money and put it in his pocket,
And de way he did put out was a sin to Davy Crocket;
So old Missis cry and 'gin to wipe her eye
For she marry Bill de weaver she cou'dn't tell why.

6

Now one day de sun gone down an' de days work over,
Old Gumbo Chaff he tink he'd live in Clover;
He jump into a boat wid his old Tamborine,
While schoonerhead Sambo play'd de Violin;

De way we sail'd to New Orleans never be forgotten,
Dey put me on de Levy dock to roll a bale of Cotton.

7

When I cotch hold de bale oh! den you ought to seen us!
First time dis child 'gan to show his genus;
I got hold de corner an' I give him such a hug,
An' light upon him like a duck 'pon a june bug,
Oh! you ought to been dare to see de Niggers laff,
For dey swore it was de debil or old Gumbo Chaff.

8

I learn'd to talk de French oh! a la mode de dancey,
Kick him shoe, tare him wool, parle vo de Francey,
Bone jaw Madamselle, Stevadors and Riggers,
Apple jack and sassafras and little Indian Niggers;
De natives laff'd and swore dat I was corn'd,
For dey neber heard sich French since dey was born'd.

9

I leab New Orleans early one day morning,
I jump'd aboard de boat jist as de day was dawning,
I hide behind de wood where de Niggers always toss'um,
And lay low like de Coon when him tries to food de Possum;
I lay dare still doe 'twas rather diffikill,
An dey did'nt find me out 'till I got to Louisville.

10

Dare Jim beats de drum and old Joe's de fifer,
An I is dat child what can read an cifer;
Twice one is five den carry six to seven,
Twice six is twenty nine and eighteen's eleven,

So 'twixt you and me its very plain to see,
Dat I learnt to play de Banjo by de double rule of three.

11

Now I 'rive on our farm on de Ohio Bluff,
An' I tink of fun an' frolick old Gumbo's had enough;
Oh! de white folks at home I very much amuse,
When I sing dis song an tell 'em all de news;
So we'd music all night an dey set up sich a laff
When I introduced de Niggers to Mrs. Gumbo Chaff.

Sich a Gitting Up Stairs[31]

On a Suskyhanner raft I come down de bay
And I danc'd, and I frolick'd, and fiddled all de way.
   Sich a gitting up stairs I never did see, &c.

Trike he to and heel—cut de pigeon wing,
Scratch gravel, slap de foot—dats just de ting.
   Sich a gitting up stairs I never did see, &c.

I went to de play, and I see'd Jim Crow,
Oh! nigger Isam den he swell, for Jim was no go!
   Sich a gitting up stairs I never did see, &c.

I look him in de face untill I make him grin,
And den I trow a backa quid an' hit him on de chin.
   Sich a gitting up stairs I never did see, &c.

Oh! I is dat boy dat know to preach a sarmont
Bout temperance and seven up an all dat kind of varmint.
   Sich a gitting up stairs I never did see, &c.

Nigger hold a meeting about de Colnization,
And dare I spoke a speech about Amalgamation!
   Sich a gitting up stairs I never did see, &c.

To Washington I go, dare I cut a swell
Cleaning gemmen's boots and ringin auction bell.
   Sich a gitting up stairs I never did see, &c.

I call on yaller Sal dat trade in sassenges,
An dare I met big Joe, which make my daner ris.
   Sich a gitting up stairs I never did see, &c.

Says I "you see dat door? just mosey, nigger Joe,
For I'm a Suskyhanner boy what knows a ting or two!"
   Sich a gitting up stairs I never did see, &c.

An den I show my science—prencz gardez vouz,
Bung he eye, break he shin, split de nose in two.
   Sich a gitting up stairs I never did see, &c.

Sal holler out—den she jump between us,
But guess he no forget de day wheyn Isam show his genus.
   Sich a gitting up stairs I never did see, &c.

Den big Joe went out, he gwoin to take de law,
But he no fool de Possum—I cut stick for Baltimore.
   Sich a gitting up stairs I never did see, &c.

Jim Crack Corn, or the Blue Tail Fly[32]

1

When I was young I us'd to wait
On Massa and hand him de plate;
Pass down de bottle when he git dry

And bresh away de blue tail fly.
  Jim crack corn I don't care,
  Jim crack corn I don't care,
  Jim crack corn I don't care,
  Ole Massa gone away.

2

Den arter dinner massa sleep,
He bid dis niggar vigil keep;
An' when he gwine to shut his eye,
He tell me watch de blue tail fly.
  Jim crack corn &c.

3

An' when he ride in de arternoon,
I foller wid a hickory broom;
De poney being berry shy,
When bitten by de blue tail fly.
  Jim crack corn &c.

4

One day he rode aroun' de farm,
De flies so numerous dey did swarm;
One chance to bite 'im on the thigh,
De debble take dat blu tail fly.
  Jim crack corn &c.

5

De poney run, he jump an' pitch,
An' tumble massa in de ditch;
He died, an' de jury wondr'd why
De verdic was de blue tail fly.
  Jim crack corn &c.

6

Dey laid 'im under a 'simmon tree,
His epitaph am dar to see:
"Beneath dis stone I'm forced to lie,
All by de means ob de blue tail fly."
    Jim crack corn &c.

7

Ole massa gone, now let 'im rest,
Dey say all tings am for de best;
I nebber forget till de day I die,
Ole massa an' dat blue tail fly.
    Jim crack corn &c.

Settin' on a Rail, or, Racoon Hunt[33]

As I walk'd out by de light ob de moon
So merrily singing dis same tune,
I cum across a big racoon
A sittin on a rail
    sitting on a rail,
    sittin on a rail,
    sittin on a rail,
Sleepin werry sound.

2

I at de Racoon take a peep
And den so softly to him creep,
I found de Racoon fast asleep,
    An pull him off de rail [repeat]
An fling him on de ground.

3

De Racoon gan to scratch an bite,
I hit him once wid all my might,
I bung he eye an spile he sight
   O Im dat child to fight, [repeat]
An heat de banjo to.

4

I fell de Racoon gin to pray,
While up de ground de Racoon lay,
But he jump up and run away,
   An soon he out ob sight [repeat]
Sittin on a rail.

5

My ole Massa dead an gone,
A dose ob poison help him on,
De debil say him funeral song,
   Oh bress him let him go [repeat]
An joy go wid him to.

6

De Racoon hunt do werry quare,
Am no touch to kill de deer
Be Case you kotch him wid out fear,
   Sittin on a rail, [repeat]
Sleepin werry sound.

7

Ob all de songs dat eber I sung,
De Racoon hunt's de greatest one,
It always pleases old and young,
   An den dey cry encore, [repeat]
An den I cum agin.

PLAYS

I edited these plays from the handwritten prompt scripts, founding decisions upon this primary question: what returns the play most closely to the way Rice's own audiences experienced it? I always preferred a fuller to a shorter play if there was evidence that he regularly performed more scenes. This volume therefore contains the fullest texts justifiable on the grounds of performance.

Virginia Mummy

A Farce in One Act[1]

Scene 1. A Room. Enter Captain Rifle *followed by* Waiter *with baggage* LH

Rifle: Let me have a commodious room, fellow; patent sofa[2], and gum elastic[3] bath.

Waiter: Yes, Sir. [*Exit* Waiter LH]

Rifle: Well, here I am once again, once more inhaling the balmy atmosphere that gives the life, the joy, the animation to my retrospections: I am afraid Lucy will scarcely know me—for a two years' campaign on our western frontier changes a man's complexion, as a chameleon does its color. I will first see if there be letters from my old dad at the Post Office. [*calling waiter; enter* Ginger Blue LH]

Ginger: Did you call me, master?

Rifle: I call'd the waiter, are you he?

Ginger: I ar one of dem.

Rifle: I ar one of dem! And how many does it take to make one of dem?

Ginger: Dar's where you hab me. I guess it take a right smart change, anyhow.

Rifle: Well, you are an original.

Ginger: No, I'm a Wirginian.

Rifle: Ha! ha! ha! Come here. Can you go an errand for me?

Ginger: If you isn't sent nobody else.

Rifle: What do you ask me that for?

Ginger: 'Cause if dere's two, we'll be sure to quarrel about de pay when we come back.

Rifle: But suppose I do not choose to pay you? What then will be the consequence?

Ginger: It will be rather hard to hear you when it rings.

Rifle: Ha! ha! He has a reason for his subtlety, but not experience enough to conceal it. Well, go you to the Post Office, and ask if there be any letters for Captain Rifle and, if so, bring them direct to me. Here, Sir, is a dollar.

Ginger: Look here, you isn't Captain Rifle dat sold Massa a load de coal?

Rifle: No, no, damn it, no; do you take me for a coal merchant? I am Captain Rifle of the Army.

Ginger: Is you a soger?

Rifle: Ask no further questions, but be gone.

Ginger: Well master, I only ax't.[4] [*Exit* Ginger Blue LH]

Rifle: I am afraid that stupid negro will make some mistake; however, it is but a stone's throw, if I have to go myself. Lucy little thinks her lover is so near, or a welcome in a shape of a billet-doux,[5] would have dropped from the point of love's own weapon. But how to procure an interview? Her guardian was opposed to me for not reconciling myself to the pestle and mortar, as he styles it. But, no, give me a soldier's life, with *one arm* and *half* a leg in preference to a stuffed Alligator, or a box of pills[6]—but should her affections have changed, oh, fie! To think it! Woman's love is like a falling torrent,[7] ever constant, and man recedes from nature's dignity when he suspects without a cause.

I'll now to my room, change my dress, and devise means to announce my arrival. [*Exit* Rifle RH]

᛭

Scene 2. Room in Galen's House. Enter Doctor Galen[8] *and* Charles LH

Charles: Here's the advertisement, and I have given orders to continue the publication 'til further notice—

Galen: That's right, let me see, "*Wanted a mummy*"—excellent. [*reads*] "*Doctor Galen being anxious to try the virtue of his new invented Compound Extract of Live-Forever upon the mortal remnants of Egypt and China, will give the highest price for embalmed mummies. For further particulars, please call at his office, Exchange Building.*" This is excellent. Now, if I can only resuscitate life that's been extinct for three thousand years—why, vanish all ye quacks and diabolical impostors! The world shall begin all anew; the glorious battles of Major Pompey and General Caesar, shall be repeated like an opera in a theatre, while I stand upon the mount of Aetna, and pour down my new invented Compound Extract of Live-Forever. [*crosses left*]

Charles: But, Sir, suppose you should try it on some person who has been dead a week, or three days, or, say, one day; and if it succeeds *then* try it on your mummies.

Galen: Why, you impudent Jackanapes;[9] you thing of no penetration, do you think I have studied for twenty-five years to procure an antidote to bring back the life of this degenerate race of mankind? No—tis for the days of King Solomon, King Pharaoh, King Brutus, and King Crusoe.

Charles: I beg your pardon, Sir, but I don't remember ever reading of King Crusoe.

Galen: Who said you did? I never read of him myself. I only heard of him.

Charles: [*aside*] Ha! Ha! Ha! What country, Sir, was this King Crusoe of?

Galen: He was from no country, but from the Norwegian Islands, and the first man that discovered America.

Charles: Well, Sir, was this three thousand years ago?

Galen: More than that, Sir, it was long before the Battle of Stonington.[10]

Charles: [*aside*] Ha! Ha! Ha!

Galen: What are you giggling at, you impudent rascal? Out of the room, out of the room this instant. [*Exit* Charles LH] What is society coming to? Impudence! And ignorance is paramount to everything! No matter. I shan't let him see me perform the operation on a mummy, nor shall he know the ingredients that I use: when I die, I shall *will* the receipt to the college to be performed on me at the expiration of One Thousand Years. Then I will publish a work on my other world peregrinations. [*Enter* Lucy LH]

Lucy: La! Guardian, what have you done to Charles? He is as scared as if he was going to be married.

Galen: An impudent blockhead: when I was diffusing into his thick skull the knowledge of philosophy, he bursts out a-laughing in my face and pays no more attention to me than if I were the cook or butler.

Lucy: Now, guardian, tell me, who is this handsome young man, you have destined for my husband?

Galen: He is a professor of zoological subjects. I saw him this morning. He was busily employed in stuffing a rhinoceros which I intend to purchase to place among my collections.

Lucy: Oh, la! To marry a man with such a profession—he's worse than a grave digger.

Galen: Science and knowledge, before profession.

Lucy: [*half aside*] I wonder where Captain Rifle is.

Galen: What's that you say? You want to know where Captain Rifle is? Dead, I hope. I would not bring *him* to life, if there were not another man in the world.

Lucy: But only consider, my dear guardian.

Galen: I won't consider anything now but mummies. So get along to your chamber, and put this love out of your head. [*Exeunt* RH]

>-<

Scene 3. A Hotel. Enter Captain Rifle, RH.

Rifle: How long that fellow stays. I have beat my brains ever since, trying to find out a plan to introduce myself, but not one can I hit upon. Ah! Here comes the fellow, at last. [*Enter* Ginger Blue LH] Why, one would have thought you went to Paris.

Ginger: Can't help what de people tink.

Rifle: Well, did you get any letters for me?

Ginger: No—dere warn't any for you, but here's an armful I buyed for wrapping paper. Maybe some of dem do.

Rifle: Zounds! Was there ever such a perplexing[11] ink bottle?

Ginger: I ax't de man, when he 'spect you goin' to hab some.

Rifle: Well, and what did he say?

Ginger: Why, he say, clear out you damn nigger, and don't ax gemman questions.

Rifle: I'm not astonished at the answer. You will give me the change, and bring the morning newspaper.

Ginger: If I don't bring dis mornin's, I will bring de oder mornin's paper.

Rifle: Bring me this morning's and no other. Here, take this for your blundering trouble.

Ginger: Tank you, Massa, but what you gwan to do wid de oder rest of it?

Rifle: Put it in my pocket. What makes you so anxious to know?

Ginger: Noting, only it might fall out.

Rifle: Do *you get out* and bring the paper. [*Exit* Ginger LH] The rascal seems to be between the two—cunning as well as stupid. Now, let me see. Shall I say a gentleman from the South wants advice? Or shall I say I am a learned Greek doctor come to reside in his neighborhood, and wish to have his countenance?[12] No—I have it—I'll say——[*Re-enter* Ginger, *with paper* LH]

Ginger: Here's de paper, Massa.

Rifle: Well, what does the paper say?

Ginger: I doesn't know, he haven't spoke a word.[13]

Rifle: Give it here! [*reads*] "*Foreign intelligence.*"

Ginger: Who is he, I wonder?

Rifle: "*Mummies wanted*" [*reads the advertisement*]. Zounds, this is Lucy's old guardian. I wonder where I can purchase a mummy? I am afraid I shall find them rather a scarce article in market. I have it. I will have a dead body dug up; then smoke it and roll it up in several old sheets, put it into a box stained with a few hieroglyphics, and I defy old Nick[14] himself to detect the cheat. Ginger, come here. Do you know where the undertaker lives?

Ginger: Who is dem?

Rifle: People who attend the funerals.

Ginger: The Lord knows, I doesn't want to know dem.

Rifle: Do you know where I could get a dead body?

Ginger: Yes, I does dat—

Rifle: Where?

Ginger: Ole Massa Sander's nigger shot a deer dis mornin'.

Rifle: No, I mean a human body.

Ginger: A human body—what's dat?

Rifle: A dead man.

Ginger: I knows where you can git a man *dead* drunk.

Rifle: Where, you stupid?

Ginger: Only you pay for de liquor—and de apparition stand right afore you.

Rifle: I can't get any information out of this fellow, I will see the landlord. Stay you here until I return. [*Exit Rifle* LH]

Ginger: I wonder what he gwan to do wid de inhuman dead body. I guess he gwan to make de doctor's stuff. I'll be mighty careful how I drink de wine at de dinner table, else when I gwan to fetch de gemmen's baggage I find myself a dead nigger. Be careful, Ginger Blue, you isn't fool'd like de white folks: get up in de mornin' and wonder why dey can't find demselves. [*Re-enter* Captain Rifle LH]

Rifle: The landlord is not in, and I have thought of a better scheme. Here, Ginger, is a silver dollar for you. How long can you hold your tongue without speaking?

Ginger: Well, I guess I hold him, 'til I git about tired.

Rifle: Can you shut your mouth—not speak without I tell you?

Ginger: Yes. Spose you tell me to speak to people I don't 'sociate wid—how I gwan to do den?

Rifle: Suppose you don't speak at all?

Ginger: Den it be de best way for me to say notin'.

Rifle: So it will. Now, listen [*Ginger goes to door*]. No, no, come here to me; I want you now to make folks believe you are a mummy.

Ginger: Who am dem?

Rifle: You don't understand me. A mummy is a dead man preserved in spices, put into a coffin, deposited in a tomb, and never molders away.

Ginger: And do you want to pickle me up in dat way? Child, de wedder is too hot! Dis ole nigger wouldn't keep from now 'til Sunday.

Rifle: I only want you to have the appearance of it, to make people think you are a mummy, when you are only Ginger Blue.

Ginger: Well, did you ebber hear de like? You is too debbily for de nigger.

Rifle: Come along after me to my room, where I will dress and paint you, and give you a lesson to show you how to keep still.

Ginger: How, is you gwan to paint me, Master, like a sign?

Rifle: No, like a mummy—white, black, green, blue, and a variety of colors.

Ginger: Massa, put plenty of turpentine wid de white paint so it won't rub off. I like to make 'em believe I'm a white man, too.[15]

Rifle: Above all, don't breathe loud.

Ginger: I mind dat, for ebery time I gwan to breath, I put my hand right up to my mouth.

Rifle: Then they will be sure to find you out.

Ginger: Nebber mind dat, I'll swear I'm a mummy.

Rifle: But you must be silent as death and, if you succeed, I will give you a five dollar note.

Ginger: Dat's a whole month's wages, but what I gwan to do when I get hungry? You know de mummies couldn't live widout dey hab de wittles.

Rifle: I will be near, and see that you do not want for anything. But you must try to remember that mummies are dead and never eat.

Ginger: Yes, but I'm a live mummy.

Rifle: Well, anyway, so you answer my purpose. Come, we have little time to lose.

Ginger: I spect you gwan to make a show of me. [*Exit* Rifle, RH]

Song—"Jim Crow"[16]

[*Exit* Ginger Blue, RH]

➤◄

Scene 4. Doctor's office. Pallette and brushes on. Charles and O'Leary discovered: Charles painting from a Boa Constrictor which O'Leary holds in his hand. Pestle and mortar on.

O'Leary: Sure, when nature molded the cratur, she had some very whimsical ideas about her when she made such a thing as this.

Charles: I have almost finish'd. Hold up the head 'til I get the color of the eye. That will do.

O'Leary: His eye is like Paddy Cape's light house, seen as well in a mist as in a fog.

Charles: What do you mean by that, you thick-skull'd rhubarb pounder.

O'Leary: Sure, is there any eye there? Isn't it shut up as close as Barney Laughlin's whiskey shop on a Sunday?

Charles: Well, lay it aside, you booby. There's as fine an imitation of an anaconda as two peas.

O'Leary: As two peas! Sure then, one of them must be in a pod.

Charles: How so?

O'Leary: Sure, isn't this one straight out, like a crook'd stick?[17] And isn't the other screw'd up, as if he had the cramp?[18]

Charles: Ha! ha! It is his common position.

O'Leary: Then it's very common, let me tell you. If you want wild animals why don't you paint a rhinosorus?

Charles: Rynosorus! Rhinoceros, you mean.

Figure 2. "Mr. T. Rice as the Original Jim Crow," *by Edward Williams Clay.*
Courtesy of the Harvard Theatre Collection, The Houghton Library.

O'Leary: Well, didn't I say rynosnorus? Och! That would be a
   beautiful subject.

Charles: Where did you ever see one?

O'Leary: I saw one in the ship I came over in. They had him hanging up in a cage with the canary bird.

Charles: Ha! ha! ha! A rhinoceros hanging up with a canary bird!

If you had told that to the sailors, they would have pitched you overboard.

O'Leary: No, they wouldn't have pitched me overboard; they wasn't so desartless of breeding as you are, Mr. Charles; they were gintlemin, as so was the Captain, and so was the steerage pasenger, Mr. O'Leary. [*turning to pestle and mortar*]

Charles: Well, but, Mr. O'Leary, I meant no offence.

O'Leary: Oh! Get out, ye dirty rattlesnake portrait painter. You aren't fit to white-wash a parish school house fince.

Charles: And instead of mixing medicines, you ought to be mixing mortar.

O'Leary: Sure, and haven't I done that already? It was there I got my hand in, or how the divil do you think I could be a doctor, and mixing up things, if I hadn't a little practice?

Charles: And a pretty doctor you are, too; you cannot tell a box of pills from a bottle of Swain's Panacea.

O'Leary: Sure, can't I taste thim, and tell by the effects they have upon the system?

Charles: Ha! ha! Was there ever such a clod? Now, O'Leary, what would you do, suppose you should see a man fall out of a garret window?

O'Leary: What would I do? Why, pick him up, to be sure.

Charles: Ha! ha! ha!

O'Leary: Ha! ha! ha! Och! You may ha! ha! Maybe, Mr. Charles, I won't tell the doctor how you want to be sweethearting Miss Lucy.

Charles: Silence! Here comes the doctor. [*Enter* Doctor Galen, LH]

Galen: Now, I shall be able to try my genius, here's a letter from a gentleman just-arrived from Grand Cairo in Upper Egypt that has a mummy taken from the Pyramids 3000 years old.

O'Leary: That's some time before I left Ireland.

Galen: Now, Charles, let the incredulous world tremble, and those who have laughed at my discovery: Down, and beg for mercy.

Charles: When will it be here?

Galen: I expect it every minute. Now, Charles, I want you, as soon as I restore its life, to be ready with pen, ink, and paper to write his history, which I intend to have translated into French, German, Latin, Greek and Choctaw.

Charles: But what language will he speak, Sir? For if it does not speak plain English, I shall not be able to understand it.

O'Leary: If it's the sweet mother tongue, just cast your eye around and you will find O'Leary close at your elbow.

Galen: I have it—go you for the learned schoolmaster who has recently opened school in the neighborhood and he shall be the one to do the business.

Charles [*aside:*] And a pretty business I'm afraid he'll make of it. [*Exit* Charles LH]

Galen: Now, let me see if everything is ready [*goes to box and takes out a large bottle*]. This is the elixir to make a marble statue speak. Now, O'Leary have every thing in its proper place—my knives, my saws, my augers, gimlets, etc.

O'Leary: Faith, everything will be as ready as the wake of Teddy Rowe.

Galen: I believe I had better add a half an ounce more of alcohol to kill the taste of the asafoetida, and you, O'Leary, get a bottle of Thompsonian No. 6 to rub him down with, in case that change of climate gives him a cold. [*Enter* Susan LH]

Susan: Doctor, breakfast is ready.

Galen: Bring it in here, I have no time now to leave the office. O'Leary remain you here to receive the mummy. [*Exit* Galen *and* Susan LH]

O'Leary: What the devil is he going to do with the mummy? Faith, Charles told me it was a dead man wrapp'd up in a napkin of molasses. I begin to think it's a big fish. [*Enter* Charles LH]

Charles: O'Leary! O'Leary, it's come, it's come, and the owner with it, who is in full dress—the original costume of his native country.

O'Leary: In full dress, the costume of his country—and isn't a full dress the costume of all countries, you Hottentot, and would you have a man go half-naked?

Charles: Now we shall see, I have often read about mummies, but never saw one. Only fancy, a man that lived 3000 years ago.

O'Leary: That's nothing—St. Patrick lived before the world was made.

Charles: Ha! ha! That's as bad as the rhinoceros and the Canary bird. Stand aside, here comes the Doctor and the owner. [*Enter* Doctor, *with bottle, and the* Captain *dress'd in a Persian dress LH—all bow to the* Captain]

Galen: Welcome, Sir, to the young world, as it is call'd in Captain Cook's life.[19]

Rifle: Sir, I thank you, and, ere we part, we will be better acquainted.

Galen: If not, Sir, then have I degenerated with society.

O'Leary: He's got a hat like a washerwoman.

Charles: And an overcoat like a short-gown.

Rifle: How many inmates have you in your house?

Galen: My wife, and my ward, Lucy, and myself. The others you see are my domestics, except this young man who is an artist and has been busily employed in painting my ward's portrait.

Rifle: Sir, I bow submissive to genius.

Galen: But come, Sir, now for inspecting the mummy—

Rifle: Handle it very careful, for it is old and unused to being in its present situation.

Galen: Come Charles, come O'Leary, don't be in too great a haste, take care! Be careful! [*Exeunt* Galen, Charles, *and* O'Leary LH]

Rifle: I see nothing of my Lucy, as yet. But, so far, so well. If blackey only keeps still, I defy them to find out the cheat. [*Enter* Galen, Charles, O'Leary LH, *with mummy*]

Galen: There now, set it down, and let it be open'd immediately. Shut the windows and the doors, so that the spicy fragrance may not escape.

[O'Leary *goes up and shuts window. All commence hammering on the sarcophagus, the* Doctor *with a hammer and chisel at the head,* Charles *and* O'Leary *at the foot*]

Ginger: [*from inside*] Look here! Look here—what de debbil is you about? [*All stagger from the sarcophagus*]

Rifle: Gentlemen! Gentlemen! What are you about?

Galen: Was it you, Mr. Egyptian? Why, I declare I thought the voice came from the coffin.

Rifle: You will knock it all to pieces, Sir. Give me the hammer. [*he opens it*]

Omnes: What a curiosity.

Galen: Don't touch it! Don't touch it: in what a perfect state of preservation! The expression of the eye has all its natural lustre.

Rifle [*aside:*] It worked well! I must continue to retire to some other apartment or I shall burst with laughter.

Galen: Mr. Egyptian, while I am trying the experiment you may amuse yourself in the garden, or library, or with the chit-chat of my ward, Lucy.

Rifle: With all my heart.

Galen: Come, Sir, I will introduce you; this way, if you please. [*Exeunt* Galen *and* Rifle RH]

O'Leary: And is that what you call a mummy? It looks for all the world like a smok'd hog.[20]

Charles: Poor fellow! He little thought, 3000 years ago, that he was to be brought here to recite the adventures of the other world. Now, while I think of it, and as I will not have a better opportunity, I'll go and get my palette, brush, and paints, and take a sketch of it. [*Exit* Charles RH]

O'Leary: Look here! Mr. Charles! Don't leave me alone with this black looking mummy! Och! Sure, and isn't he dead, and what the devil should I be afraid of? I wonder where the doctor is, eh! He's with the gentleman that pickled him. By the powers, what would Mrs. O'Leary say if she was just to have a squint at it? There's nobody nigh. I'll just take my knife and cut off the big toe, and send it in a letter to her. [*As he is about to cut off the toe, the mummy raises his right foot and kicks him over.*]

Ginger: Not as you knows on.

O'Leary: Murther! murther—I'm kilt! I'm kilt by a dead man. [*Exit* O'Leary LH]

Ginger: Whoo! Here I is, pack'd up like a box of sugar; I guess dey tought dey was breakin' into de ballroom when dey took de kivver off. I wish some of de niggers could see me now, dey'd take me for old Santa Claus. Well, I don't like dis laying down all de time. Spose I jis stand him up dat fashion. I guess dat old Irishman, dat want to cut my toe off, must hab tought dat I had de cramp in de leg. I wonder whar de Captain is? Dis must be de doctor's shop. I wonder if I've time to run out and get someting to drink, I don't see nobody comin'. First let me look about. Hallo! What's dis? Dis must be de whiskey [*smells and drinks*]. 'Tis whiskey! I spose de mummies used to drink de whiskey like de oder folks. If I only had a little sugar, I'd make a sort of whiskey toddy. Hallo, what's dis? [*Takes down a box of lozenges*] Dis must be sugar. Now I'll hab a big drink [*drinks*]. Hallo! Somebody comin'. I must git into the sugar trough again. I'm like a Philadelphy watchman. I've got a whole box[21] to myself [*gets into box*]. [*Enter* Charles *with palette, etc.*]

Charles: Now for a sketch. Ah, O'Leary has raised it up.

Ginger: What de debbil is he gwan to do?

Charles: I'm afraid I won't be able to hit the dark shades of the face.

Ginger: As long as he don't hit me on de shin, I don't care.

Charles: But, as close as my genius will admit of, I will come to it.

Ginger: Dat save me trouble of comin' to you.

Charles: But I can scarcely realize that it lived 3000 years ago.

Ginger: Eh! eh! Honey, you're right only half of it.

Charles: No doubt it was some great personage, and stood very high in his native country.

Ginger: When I was up de tree—arter de possum.

Charles: Probably a King—

Ginger: Yes, wid a -dom come to it.

Charles: That has led triumphant armies across the plains of Egypt after the retreating enemy.

Ginger: As rader a pack of dogs troo de canebrake arter de bear.

Charles: Now contrast his situation: from a splendid palace to a domicile of drugs and medicines.

Ginger: So I see by dat bottle dare.

Charles: He might have been an artist, and handled the brush.

Ginger: 'Twas a white-wash brush den.

Charles: Or an astronomer, and read the stars.

Ginger: Well, if I did, I guess de book was upside down.

Charles: Or had an ear for music.

Ginger: Jus' gin me a banjo—dat's all.

Charles: Oh! What a field imagination may trace to find out what it is.

Ginger: You put me in a corn *field,* I show what it is.

Charles: I wonder if his race were all that color?

Ginger: I guess you find me a pretty fair sample.

Charles: And such a prodigious height—almost a giant.

Ginger: Yes, almost, but not quite.

Charles: I wonder what his name was?

Ginger: Ginger Blue, all de world ober.

Charles: But that I suppose is mark'd on the coffin.

Ginger: I guess you'll hab to spose it.

Charles: There *are* figures, but I cannot make them out. I would like to touch it; there can be no harm in that. How soft and moist the flesh is, and quite warm. How confoundedly it smells of shoe blacking.[22] I would like to have a finger to keep as a curiosity. I'll just clip one off. No doubt this hand held a sceptre with as firm a grasp as Samson did when he let fall ... [Ginger *butts him on the head*—Charles *falls*] Murder! Murder! Murder. [Charles *gets up and runs off* LH]

Ginger: Yah! Yah! I guess he won't want anoder finger in a hurry. Dese white folks must all be crazy. Dey talk like de Indians do when dey don't know what to say. I know one ting, I begin to feel pretty hungry, and if de Captain don't come soon, I'll break and put out. Ah! Here he come. [*Enter* Rifle RH]

Rifle: Hallo! Ginger, what are you doing out of the box?

Ginger: I'm arter some cold vittles, is you got any?

Rifle: You shall have some presently, get back into the box; I hear some one coming. I have disclosed myself to Lucy, and she will be ready in an hour, to elope with me. What are you doing there?

Ginger: I'm arter some liquor.

Rifle: Quick! Ginger! Quick! [*Enter* Galen *with a bag of instruments*, RH]

Galen: Ah! Mr. Egyptian, I see you have stood it up. So much the better; I can pour the extract down with greater facility.

Ginger: Dis is de ole fellow, I wonder what he gwan to do?

Rifle: Keep still, you rascal.

Galen: But tell me Mr. Egyptian, what do you think of my ward?

Rifle: She is beautiful!

Galen: She has a fortune to back that beauty. I say nothing, but she had her eye on you all the time.

Rifle: Oh! Sir!

Galen: I'll speak a good word for you, and you must manage the affair yourself.

Rifle: Thank you, Sir, I think I had better join her again.

Galen: Certainly, by all means [*Exit* Rifle RH] I must put a little more alcohol in this to weaken it—for two drops is enough to kill a person [*Ginger very uneasy*]—as it is now in its present condition *rank* poison; nothing could save a man.

Ginger: Den I'm a gone case.

Galen: I'll just step and prepare it, and then be back and try my experiment. [*Exit* Galen RH]

Ginger: Oh, de Lord! I'm gone now! What de debbil did I drink dat stuff for? It will kill me! Oh, de Lord! I'm gwan to die, den I will be a mummy for sartain [*falls on his knees and begins to pray; enter* Susan *with the tray & breakfast,* LH]

Susan: Master told me to bring his breakfast here; now I'll have a peep at the mummy [*Sees Ginger; screams and runs off* LH; *lets the tray fall*[23]]

Ginger: [*Jumps up and goes into box*] O, de debbil! Who's dat? Scream like a cat bird. [*Re-enter* Susan LH]

Susan: Oh me! How scared I am! I thought it was in a box. So it is; who could it have been that I saw kneeling there on the floor? Oh, I expect it was O'Leary trying to frighten me. What a timid creature I am, to be sure, frightened at my own shadow. Oh, my! What an ugly thing it is [*starts*] I thought it moved its eye. Pshaw! I won't be afraid. There—I should like to touch it. I will just put my finger in its mouth. [*Ginger bites her finger. She screams and runs round the room, Ginger following.*]

Ginger: Look here—look here—[*Exit* Susan LH] I cocht de finger in de trap like dey do de wolf. Ha! I smell someting good, dat's de ole doctor's breakfast. I mean to light on it for fear I don't hab anoder opportunity. I'm just about as hungry as a fish hawk— go right in ober head. I wish I had bite dat woman's finger off. I make her gib me a dollar 'fore I gib it back to her. Oh, de Lord! White sugar! [*empties the contents in his pocket*] I lay for de storm. Now I eat enough, I put de rest into de box, in case I hab de appetite. [*Enter* Rifle RH]

Rifle: Come, Ginger. Ginger! Here comes the doctor.

Ginger: Look here, Captain, I want to go home. I've been drink de doctor's stuff out of dat bottle. I afraid I'm gwan to die.

Rifle: Never fear, allay your apprehensions, for the contents of that bottle is nothing but whiskey and water. I took most especial care in pouring out the original elixir and substituting whiskey and water.

Ginger: Well, if dat's de case, I'm saucy Ginger Blue again.

Rifle: Never mind, keep still.[24] [*Exit* Rifle LH; *enter* Doctor Galen RH *shaking a bottle*]

Galen: Now for the great experiment.

Ginger: If I drink all dat, I guess I'll be tight.

Galen: But first, I'll eat my breakfast. Hallo! Can I have eaten my breakfast? There's nothing here but empty dishes. I'll be bound, that fellow O'Leary has eat it for me. Zounds, he does nothing but eat, sleep, and drink. He has not only devoured the trout, eggs, and coffee but he has eaten up all the sugar.[25]

Ginger: How would you like to hab a lump?

Galen: No matter, I'll have a better appetite for my dinner.

Ginger: And if you isn't, I'll help you.

Galen: There you are, illustrious stranger, cold and silent as a block of marble.

Ginger: Why, I'm sweating like a race horse.

Galen: You little think that Dr. Galen is standing before you.

Ginger: Or you little tink dat Ginger Blue is standing behind you.

Galen: But before I bow with reverence as Solomon did before Great Sheba—

Ginger: De same, to you, I hope you berry well.

Galen: Could you but speak, what scenes you would relate about your ancestors, and wonders would you tell to this world, what happened in yours!

Ginger: I'd tell you who eat up your breakfast.

Galen: Those lips, that look so parch'd and dry, perhaps did seal the nuptial kiss to some fair Princess, chaste and fair as the lilly beams of Bright Aurora.

Ginger: De only Prince he kiss was old Aggs, and she's as black as de debbil.

Galen: Where now are your friends that mourned your loss, that saw you embalmed, and saw you laid in the mighty hetacombs[26] of Egypt?

Ginger: I guess some of dem gwan down de river[27]—oh! Eh!

Galen: Not one even to give a nod, but all gone from whence they came.

Ginger: I want to be gwan, ole Massa'll be looking for me.

Galen: But you shall be resuscitated.

Ginger: What de debbil does he mean by suscitate?

Galen: And marry my ward.

Ginger: Dat's what de missionary call de 'malgamation.[28]

Galen: To inject my elixir, I will have to bore a hole in his head;

Ginger: Oh, Lord! Den all my brains come out.

Galen: Or, as the ancient professors did, open an artery [*taking up a large knife*].

Ginger: Oh, de debbil! He's gwan to cut me up like de fig!

Galen: And if that will not do, I'll sew up his mouth and lance him in the back of his neck.

Ginger: Den I had better make haste and eat dis bone.

Galen: However, I shall try every experiment to be fully satisfied of its virtue.[29] [*Enter* O'Leary LH]

O'Leary: Here's a gentleman that has brought another of these pickled mummies, or what do you call 'em.

Galen: Show him in. [*Exit* O'Leary LH] I'll try the experiment on all they bring. Now, if I fail on this mummy, I will be sure to hit it on the other. [*Re-enter* O'Leary, *with* Charles *and* Mr. Patent LH]

O'Leary: By the powers, we'll have a whole army of mummies, by-and-by.

Galen: Stand it up along side of this one. [*They open it*] It has a much older appearance than the first one.

Patent: It has been roughly handled by the sailors on board the ship.

O'Leary: It looks like a dried herring.

Galen: O'Leary, go, and bring the Egyptian. [*Exit* O'Leary RH] And Charles you go and bring Lucy, to see the operation.

Charles: Yes, and get my pencil ready to take the expression while it's dead. [*Exit* Charles RH]

Galen: [*To Patent*] Come, sir, you must want some refreshment. Step this way. [*Exeunt* Galen *and* Patent LH]

Ginger: [*Looking about*] How do you do? Oh! You don't talk like a Virginny Mummy. I wonder whar dey git him. He look like a burnt chuck.[30] I spect dey git him out of de bee-gum.[31] I 'gin to feel berry dry. I guess I take some ob dis, de Captain said he mix him himself. It's too strong ob de water. [*Drinks out of the bottle*] Look here you hab some. Ha! I drink for you myself. I guess if de chap wants to cut off my toe he want to cut off your leg, can't help youself neider. I wonder whar de Captain is? He said he wouldn't be out ob de way, when I wanted him. I hope he ain't run away, and left me all alone. Dey'll be sure to kick me into a real mummy. I begin to feel like de appetite. [*Eats*] I can't help but laugh how de old man look when de breakfast was all gone. He was rather jubious[32] wedder *he* eat it or *not*. I guess I take a little more liquor becase if dey pickle de mummy in de liquor dey ought to put some ob de liquor *in* de mummy. Oh! Here dey all come. [*Gets into box. Enter* Dr. Galen *and* Patent LH; Charles, Rifle, Lucy, O'Leary RH]

Ginger: Dey are gwan to hab Camp Meeting.

Galen: Now, Mr. Patent, I shall begin with you first.

Ginger: Guess dat aren't strong enough.

Rifle: Silence, be quiet.

Galen: I shall first pour it down the throat to warm the system before I open the arteries. He doesn't speak, as yet.

Rifle: Now try mine.

Galen: [*Placing funnel and pouring the liquor*] See! It winks! It moves.

Rifle: Give it some more.

Galen: See, it walks! It moves! Look! Look! [*Running about the stage—Ginger following*]

Omnes: 'Tis brought to life—it lives! It lives!

Galen: Now, Mr. Egyptian, ask me for anything! Everything, you shall have it!

Rifle: The hand of your ward.

Galen: Take her, and all her fortune—likewise a bottle of this elixir, which I will prepare. The world shall now acknowledge me! Most reverend mummy, what shall I order for your dinner?

Ginger: I isn't hungry 'case I eat up all de breakfast.

Charles: [*Seizing him*] Curse me if it isn't Ginger Blue, the nigger that lives at the hotel.

Galen: Old Ginger Blue—and are you not a mummy?

Ginger: Not myself, Sar, damn if I am.

O'Leary: Ooh! What a cursed scrape I'd got into, if I had cut his toe off!

Galen: Get me a gun, I will shoot him.

Ginger: What? After bowing before me, as King Solomon did before de She nigga?[33]

Galen: And you, Sir, who are you?

Rifle: Captain Rifle, and soon will be your ward's husband.

O'Leary: Here comes the schoolmaster, who is to write the life of the mummy. [*Enter* Schoolmaster LH]

Galen: Write the life of the devil! [*Beats O'Leary offstage; knocks Schoolmaster down; paces up and down the stage in a rage.*] I'm mad enough to pound you all into a mummy, and then myself.

Ginger: Den I gib you some ob dis, to reconsuscitate you wid.

Charles: Come, doctor, love has no bounds—prithee, forget and forgive.

Galen: But I shall be laughed at by the whole town.

Rifle: What signifies the folly of the town, so long as you can retrieve the mummy.

Galen: Well, I do forget and forgive; and the next time I try my experiment on a mummy—

Ginger: I hope you make de medicine strong. And should any ob de faculty hab occasion for a libe mummy again, dey hab only to call on Ginger Blue; when dey'll find him ready dried, smoked, and painted, to sarbe himself up at de shortest notice.

Bone Squash

A Burletta[1]

Cast of Characters

Bone Squash
Spruce Pink
Jim Brown
Mose
Juba
Caesar
Pompey Duckellegs[2]
Sam Switchell, the Yankee Devil
Amos
Janson
Junietta Duckellegs
Janza Snowball
Milly
    Black Ladies, Niggers, Sweeps, Watchmen

Scenes
Act 1

Scene 1, the corner of a street—grog shop. Scene 2, a street. Scene 3, a house.

Act 2

Scene 1, a street. Scene 2, a cellar in the Five Points. Scene 3, exterior of a barber shop. Scene 4, interior of barber shop in confusion. Scene 5, a street. Scene 6, the whole stage.

Properties

Violin for Brown. Long Pole, with dirty boots, for Mose. Brushes, scrapers. Two boys: blankets and bags for boys. Whitewash pail and long pole for Juba. Patent sweeper brush, etc, for Bone Squash. Red fire. Bottles and glasses. Lobster. Dice box. Barrels. Devil's Tail. Money. Basket. Check for Devil.

Bone Squash

Act 1

Scene 1. *Curtain rises to slow music. The corner of a street. Grog shop underneath a cellar. A wheelbarrow, L.H. Pail with whitewash beside the door. Dark stage.* Caesar *lying asleep in wheelbarrow.*

Enter Jim Brown *from house.* Caesar *awakes from the barrow. Enter* Mose *and* Juba *from house. Enter* Amos *from cellar. Each character to make himself visible about the last line of the preceding verse. During 3rd verse,* Watchman *enters, L.H. and exits R.H. During 4th verse, the window in shop is opened—a barrel filled with brooms is placed at door. Over door a sign—*"Large bread for sale here." *The* Watchman, *previous to his going off, puts out light in lamp. The business in this scene is very particular, as there is no symphony between the verses of the solos.*

Enter Jim Brown *from house with fiddle.*

Jim Brown:

Oh, hurrah, day's breaking, oh!
Oh, hurrah, day's breaking, oh!
I'll put up my fiddle
And go home to bed.
For my head like de debil am aching.
Oh! [*retires,* R.]

Mose:

We're gwine to hab rain, dat's comfort, oh!
We're gwine to hab rain, dat's comfort, oh!
De boots must be black'd

And de shoes must be brush'd,
Else de gemmen won't feel like a dandy, oh!
Amos [*to two young sweeps, who come out as he calls them*]:
Come, gather up out ob de cellar, oh!
Come, gather up out ob de cellar, oh!
   Dar's chimnies to sweep
   And you're both fast asleep,
And not the first cent for your breakfast, oh!
Juba:
I'm de Nigger dat do de whitewashing, oh
I'm de Nigger dat do de whitewashing, oh
   On de scaffold I stand
   Wid de brush in my hand
And de genus shines out wid de slashing, oh.[3]
[*All join in general chorus, repeating the last verse*]

Jim Brown: Ha, ha, ha! I cannot help my facetious humor to meditate how natur hab rabished her conneasticle endowments upon de human family. Now, for example, while she make me de great musiciana, she only make you a common mechanic. From de fiddle to de base drum, I am what de white folks call *deficient en-mass.*

Juba: Look here, Mr. Brown, I don't know what you mean by deficient on de bass drum and de fiddle, for I'm one ob dem Niggers dat nebber blow my own trumpet; but you gib me de side wall ob de church, and though I isn't de portrait painter, jist gib me my whitewashing brush, and if de genus doesn't shine out like raccoon from a woodpile, say I can't slacken de lime, dat's all.

Caesar: Look here, Mr. Juba, I'm one ob dose colored gemmen dat nebber says anyting. But when I hear Niggers blazing what dey gwan to do, it always puts me in mind, as if dar was two selfs to a

Nigger; the one self did all de work, while de oder self talk about it. But if you jist gib me de gemmen's baggage straight for de City Hotel, and if you don't see a wheelbarrow go by steam, take me up for running on de walk. [*Crosses to* R.H.]

Amos: Well, I must confess, when Niggers introduce wheelbarrows to 'nopolize de conversation, s'ciety am comin' to a pretty spear. I've seen de time when de chronometar was twenty foots below freena, and de fire shake like a frosty mornin' wid de cold. I've seen dem two little jubenile sweeps throw down more cindars dan a Christmas hail storm. [*Retires up.*]

Mose: Well, never mind, gib me a box of Warren's patent shoe blacking, a little old Tom to grease my elbow, and de gemmen I black boots for travel with his own looking glass. [*All laugh.*]

Jim Brown: Your ideas are so indirectly ober de way from one another, owing to your professions, dat it puts me in mind ob de Park orchestra, trying to play on overture.[4] The horn takes up de superana, de triangular takes up de alto, and leab nothing but de solo for de bass drum. And in condition to dat, hear what de great doctor ob Physgne Combobologist say: he says, dat on de back of de head, just in de middle ob de craneum, de organ ob music am very strongly enveloped in de great Paganini.[5] Now, I've got a bump dar, big as de great watermelon.

Mose: How did you get dat bump? Buttin' down de fence?

Jim Brown: No, natur gib em to me. Buttin' down de fence?—what you take a musiciana for, you saucy Nigger? Now, leff me feel your head; you isn't got no bump like de one I is. You is got a berry big bump, just oder de ear. And dat's de sign you black de boots. [*All laugh*]

Caesar: What is dis bump I got here?

Jim Brown: Dat is de bump what holds de brains. [*Feeling his own head.*] I isn't got dat myself.

Caesar: Why, how you keep your head in shape?

Jim Brown: Why, when natur make me, he make me all for music.
So, you see, de brains hab to gib way for de music.

Song

Air, "I Am de Paganini"[6]

I am de Paganini
And my name's Jim Brown,
I fiddle at de Five Points,
And all about de town.
I plays upon de banjo,
And I beats de brass drum,
Stands upon de clarionet,
B., number one.

    Chorus:

    I am de Paganini
    And my name's Jim Brown
    I fiddle at de Five Points,
    And all about de town

        [*All dance the shuffle*]

Dar's music in de horse shoe,
And in de tin pan,
Music in de cross-bow,
Dat few understan'
Dar's music in de kettle,
When it's boiling on de fire,
Music in all natur,
Jim Brown nebber tire.

    Chorus

[All *dance and exit*, L.H. *Exit* Caesar *with wheelbarrow*, R.]
Enter Bone Squash *with a ring of wire, brush, &c. at back.*

Bone Squash: Sweep oh! Sweep oh! Twelve o'clock and no chimney yet! I've been way up Broadway, down de National Theatre, round de Coffee House Slip, and up again, and am merrier now den when I first started. I wish de debil had de man what first discovered de coal fires. I doesn't understand de chemistry ob de 'gredients 'nuff to disqualify dem; but no sooner den de coal smoke get in de chimney, den he right away emigrate out ob de top, and 'waporates into de native element like——. He doesn't adherify to de sides like de wood smoke does. I 'spect when dey make de coal, dey put in de hydrophobia gas to sort a kind o'purify it. I doesn't know what I shall do; I 'gin to feel de 'pression in de money market 'siderable. I fear I ab to jine de temperance s'ciety 'gainst my will. I hab a good notion to turn preacher. Ah, but den I hab to marry in de white families, and become demalgamated! Eh! eh! dat I neber do. I wish I could sell myself to de debil. What? Whew! Wouldn't I cut a swell in Broadway on a Sunday afternoon! Wouldn't de Anthony Niggers stare! I stand on two corners at once, and a little round into Broadway. But I wish I was de debil. Ha, ha, ha! I can't help but laugh to tink. I wish I was de debil! de idea kind o' so coincidence wid my fertile imaginations like. Ha, ha, ha!

Song

Oh, I wish I could sell myself to de debil
I'd cut a splash to kill old people.
I wish I could sell myself to de debil,
   And leff off patent sweeping.
   I'll go an buy a suit of clothes,
   Ruffle shirt and ro'cco shoeses,
   Strip cravat, whitewashed hat,
   And spectacles for de noses.
Oh, I wish I could sell myself to de debil
Crowd in, move off, and pass thro' them all.

Oh, I wish I could sell myself to de debil,
Oh, I wish I could sell myself to de debil,
   And leff off sweeping chimnies.
  Wid de brush and soap,
  So white I'd scrub me,
  Den ladies all would fall and hug me,
  Some would cry and roll dar eye,
  "Oh, de soul, I wish he'd hug me."
Oh, I wish I could sell myself to de debil,
Crowd in, move off, and pass thro' them all.

Oh, I wish I could sell myself to de debil,
Oh, I wish I could sell myself to de debil,
   New York couldn't hold me.
  At de fancy ball,
  You'd see dis child dar!
  I gib a dollar note,
  Jist to hold my coat,
  To clar de ballroom out dar.
Oh, I wish I could sell myself to de debil,
Crowd in, move off, and pass thro' them all.

The symphony is kept up till the hogshead opens, when the orchestra gives one crash with the help of the gong, and the Devil *rises. Maroon bursts.* Bone *falls and shakes violently on his back. Appropriate music, gently receding—lights up gradually.*

Devil: Howdy do? Rather guess I heard you say you wanted to see me. Well, here I am, piping hot. How do you like me? Come, gab out; don't show the Injin: let your legs fall down while your body runs away. Why, you're like a frost-bitten crane: you don't know whither to stand up or fall down. Guess you haven't made up your mind, yet.

Bone Squash: I say, is you de debil?

Devil: Yes, a real genuine Yankee devil, or a devil of a Yankee: you may have me either way by paying the discount. Don't believe I'm very particular, rather think not. However, won't be certain. What do you think?

Bone Squash: Why, I'm thinking, What de debil does you want here?

Devil: Come to buy up stock. Sartin sure I heard you say you'd like to sell out.

Bone Squash: Oh, hush!

Devil: Why, how the critter talks. Why, you're like the chap that didn't know when he was hungry, so he always eat beforehand. Well, I am a real fourth-proof devil, and one of the best in the lot.

Bone Squash: What's dat? what's dat? Best in the lot! Why, how many is there ob you?

Devil: Why, I rayther guess there's a mighty smart chance of us when we all muster. Some of them have gone to 'tend on the House of Lords, and some of them have gone down into Russia to keep an eye upon the Emperor, and others are gone to trade, that is, to swap and bargain with the missionary preacher; that's easily done. Them fellows are like a rat with your foot upon his tail, he'll skin and cut, and clear out when he's hard run. Now, some of your New York quality won't keep patience, without they have a whole devil to themselves.

Bone Squash: A whole debil to themselves! Well, how many does de Nigger hab?

Devil: Why, that's according to the quantity of wood he take. If he belongs to the temperance society, we put a devil to every two, and plenty of Newcastle coal; but if he's a real double distilled swell head, he'll burn a fortnight without any fuel, and can take care of himself. After that, we keep him for a torch, to hang in the hall. You'd do for a patent chandelier.

Bone Squash: Oh, de debil! Bone Squash, de patent sweeper, transmogrified into a patent chandelier. How de Niggers would laugh if dey was to hear dat.

Devil: Come, what do you say, you brick dust? How will you trade? You're as long striking a bargain as a Yankee and a Jew would be in swapping their conscience.

Bone Squash: Look here, Mr. Yankee debil, I'm no common Nigger what you meet wid round de market and de wharfs. I'm a gemman of color what libs wid de sweat ob de chin, as de poet says; and if you buy me you must crowd steam and come up to de landing pretty sarcy. You see, I'm a free Nigger.

[*Crosses,* L.H.]

Devil: What? a free Nigger? Well, let's see you move again! [Bone *crosses to* R.H.] Well, I rather think you are worth a couple of hundred dollars.

Bone Squash: Well, I rather tink I'm worth a couple ob dem.

Devil: Not as you knows on.

Bone Squash: Well, den I knows one ting—

Devil: What's that?

Bone Squash: I'm off like a ferry boat, when dey cross on de lag.[7] [*Going*]

Devil: Stop! Why, you damned Nigger, you're jist like a salmon— you give one nibble, and right off. I'll tell you what we'll do. I'll give you three, and split the difference; that's more than I'd give for an Indian preacher.

Bone Squash: Well, I s'pose you'll stand the liquor, too?

Devil: Well, get us a pen, ink, and paper, and I'll draw up a bond. You'll have to be your own witness.

Bone Squash: Bery well. You jist lumber here till I gwan in and fetch some. [*Exit*, R]

Devil: Well, if these Niggers ain't the softest ninnies I ever had dealings with. They're like a batch of nothing, touched with a kind of a thing, and it falls into what-you-may-call it. Darned crittur! I don't think he's got brains enough to put a stocking on inside out. Why he's worth five hundred if he's worth a Bushel of Peas.

Re-enter Bone, R.

Bone Squash: Here's de paper. Isn't got any ink, so I brought a Box of Warren's blacking—guess dat will do.

Devil: Where's de pen?

Bone Squash: Isn't got no pen neider.

Devil: Well, let's have the paper. [Bone *hands him* The Hawk and Buzzard] What's this?

Bone Squash: No, stop; don't take dat; dat's de *Hawk and Buzzard.* I patronize dat paper for 'ticular reasons; it seminates de useful knowledge to de gubernal branches ob de community.[8] Dat's de *New York Mirror;* you may hab dat. I only takes dat paper out ob compliment to de ladies.[9]

Devil: [*Dips his tail into blacking, and writes.*] Can you write?

Bone Squash: Yes, and cipher, too.

Devil: Well, let's see what your name is.

Bone Squash: Well, gib me de money fust.

Devil: First, let me know your name.

Bone Squash: Dar it is—Bone Squash!

Devil: There's the rhino.[10]

Bone Squash: What's dis? A check?

Devil: Yes, and any of the brokers will cash it.

Bone Squash: I doesn't deal in paper. I want de real buttons. Isn't you got any of de hard cash? Come, dump up.

Devil: Why I tell you it will pass on 'change like an omnibus. They all know me; I've dealings with all of them. Mention my name and any of 'em will take old Nick's check in less time than you'd light a match.

Bone Squash: Come, let's hab de liquor, and den I'm off to de tailors.

[Devil *puts bond into his pocket.* Bone *pockets the check.*]

Duet

Bone Squash:

> I'm beginning for to fill,
> Like a Baltimore Clipper.

Devil:

> But first before you go,
> Guess you'd better have the liquor.

Bone Squash:

> I'll do dat ting
> Wid de greatest ob pleasure.

Devil:

> Then get into Wall Street.
> They'll shell out the treasure.

Bone Squash:

> And ebery Nigger dat I meet,
> I'll stop him in de street
> And I'll up wid a penny,
> Head or tail for a treat.[11]

Chorus as Duet

Devil:

> I reckon now you know me,
> You can read me like a book, sir.

Bone Squash:

> You're like a singed cat,
> Much better than you look, sir.

Devil:

> But clothes, you know,
> Never make the gentleman.

Bone Squash:

> Dat am a fact,
> Or I'd been a sort ob one.

Devil:

> Only shut up your mug,
> Till the cash you hug.
> Then you'll open right upon 'em
> Like a Georgia cotton bug.[12]
> [*Chorus and dance. Exeunt* Devil, R.H., Bone, L.H.]

→←

Scene 2. A street in New York. Enter Spruce Pink *and* Junietta, *with a parasol,* R.H. *Light stage.*

Spruce: Well I neber 'sperienced such condensed wedder. De transcending streaks ob de bright effulminating sun pours down upon me like de watery element of de shower bath.

Junietta: My lub, de reason am berry perspicuous. Yesterday, de inky clouds overhung de earth as black as de smoke around de bakehouse; darfore, de heat could not perforate; but in de rotundity ob natur, dem inky clouds hab all distinguished away, and heat dat we ought to hab come down yesterday, we 'spect we hab today; consequently, we hab two days heat in one.

Spruce: By de by, I did not tink ob dat. But come, my lub, let us take some lemonade wid de sassyparilla in it, for if we stand here communicating in de sun, we'll be tanned as black as de common white folks.

Junietta: Anywhere, my dear, for de warm wedder hab so opened de paws of my system dat de perspiration flows jist as copiously as de 'lasses from de hogshead.

Spruce: Dat's a bery good sign.

Junietta: What, my lub?

Spruce: I mean de perspiration, for Dr. Johnson says, you keep de head warm, and de foots cold, and de system will always be lassitudinated.

Junietta: Oh, Mr. Pink, look at dat man on de corner! He actly got a segar in his mouth. Stop till I put dat down in my journal. [*writes*] Mr. Pink, how you spell segar.

Spruce: Che—s-e. Ghar—g-a-r. Segar.

Junietta: Tank you! I always put down ebery 'diculous custom of de white folks. Well, let's go, Mr. Pink, and when I cum back I want to make explahation from de African language.

Spruce: Suffer me. [*Takes parasol and they are about to exit*]
                    Enter Mose, *with a stick of boots.*[13]

Mose: Why, de laud a mercy, Spruce, when did you ribe from Philadelphy?

Spruce: You are mistaken in de person black man, dis 'nt he.

Junietta: Who does the impertinent Nigger mean, my lub?

Spruce: He tinks I am de gemmen he blacks de boots for.

Mose: Why look here, Spruce, you is rather lofty. I 'spect the New York climate greases wid you?

Spruce: I tell you, you must be sun struck, else you learn better how to 'sault a gemman in company wid de fair sex.

Junietta: Mr. Pink, don't excommunicate wid de Nigger any more! De people will tink you sosheate wid dem.

Mose: Now, old Spruce, you can't fool dis child. I know you as sure as I knowed a box of Warren's blacking. Who is you waiting on now?

Spruce: On de ladies, to be sure.

Mose: Is you leff off scouring?

Spruce: I'll scour you, you audacity black man.

Junietta: Stop, Mr. Pink, till I put dis down in my journal. August 32nd, 'saulted in Broadway, by common black man.

Mose: Who do you call black man?

Spruce: You, you common Nigger. [*Crossing to* Mose, *but is held back by* Junietta.]

Trio

Spruce:

> Let me go, don't hold me fast,
> I'll run that Nigger through.

Junietta:

> Oh, Mr. Pink, I really tink,
> De Nigger must be blue.

Mose:

> Oh, let him come; I'll neber run.

Spruce:

> Did you eber hear de like?

Junietta:

> Oh, pray, keep cool, don't be a fool.

Mose:

> Put up dat sword, don't strike!

[Spruce *and* Junietta *sing the first part as chorus, while* Mose *holds his sides, and laughs heartily all through.*]

Junietta:

> Brack man, I tink you'd better go.
> His passion 'gin to rise.

Mose:

> If de Nigger draws de sword agin,
> I'll slap him 'cross de eyes.

Figure 3. "A Dead Cut," from the series *Life in Philadelphia*, by Edward Williams Clay. Courtesy of The Library Company of Philadelphia.

Spruce:

      What's dat I hear?

Junietta:

      Noting, my dear.

Spruce:

      I'll make him eat his words.

Mose:

      Spell "Abel" fust![14]

Spruce:

      I almost bust.
      Your conduct is absurd.

[*Chorus as before. When within the last two bars of chorus,* Caesar *enters,* L., *with wheelbarrow, and exclaims* "Old Hays is coming."[15] *Music hurry. All scamper off.* Mose *trips up* Spruce. Caesar *wheels the barrow over him. All go off laughing at* Spruce.]

➤◄

Scene 3. Pompey Duckelleg's *house. Two chairs—music.*
Enter Junietta *in confusion.*

Junietta: I am almost horrified wid chagrin! 'Sulted by a common black man to de disgustion of Mr. Pink. I wonder where he am? Maybe dat wheelbarrow, when he ran ober him, hab dissecterated his leg, or shoulder arm. [*A knock,* L.H.] Ah! Who is dat? Should dat be Mr. Pink, and my dear fader not at home! I tremble like a catfish for de consequence. [*Knocking*] Ah, again! Ye Gods, decide my fate. [*Music. She opens the door,* L.F. *when* Pompey *enters with basket and lobster, covered*] My dear, dear fader! Whar am you been?

Pompey: Juni, dear, I am jist come from de market.

Junietta: [*aside*] My tears once more am hush'd up still. What am you buy'd my fader?

Pompey: I hab buy'd dat, my child, which am illustratious ob de wile sinner. Behold dis lobster! It am now dressed in de penitent suit ob sackcloth and ashes; but when you put him in de pot, and squeeze de kiver down upon 'em, de devil will boil out ob dem, and he'll hab de vegetated colors ob de rainbow, singed round wid de indigo ob natur.

Junietta: Bery much like de 'flection ob Mr. Pink! What else is you got?

Pompey: I got anoder ting dat my old gums smack togedder at,

like a cellar door leff off de hinges. It is de emblem ob Old Virginny, neber tire: it am de coon.

Junietta: Dis de coon?

Pompey: Dat same old coon.

Junietta: It are de coon.

Pompey: It is de coon. [*Chord. Shows it.*] It puts me in mind ob de
many moonshiney nights, when I used to go out wid de old San-
cho, and kill 'em. I buy dat coon for your wedding supper.

Junietta: [*Faints.*] Oh, my dear fader!

Pompey: What de matter wid my darter?

Junietta: Oh, my dear fader, when you talk to me—

Pompey: Sit down, my dear, I 'splain de matter. Today, I meet Bone
Squash. Fortune hab smiled upon him, and he ax me once more
to gib my darter's hand. I hab told him I will do dat ting. As
soon as he hab done wid de tailor, he will come to claim his
bride.

Junietta: It neber can—it neber shall be. Sooner den be Mistress
Squash, dat hateful, vulgar name, I exile to Siberia, and live
among de Indians. I make de solemn vow to lub Spruce Pink;
dey shall not jerk me from him. See, de wheelbarrow gwan ober
him! Old Hays hab got him—he hollers for his Junietta in vain
—she cannot help him—her cruel fader marry her to Bone
Squash! Ha! ha! ha! [*Faints.*]

        Enter Bone Squash, *in full dress,* L.H. *Chord*

Bone Squash: Hallo! What's de matter? Is de chimney afire?

Pompey: No, but my darter was so bery impatient to see you
and—

Junietta: De intensity ob de sun was so killing hot today, dat it like
to strike me dead when I was up in Broadway, and when I hear
your romantic name—

Pompey: Dar, dat is all! Dat's all explained.

Junietta: Mr. Squash, you must draw a prize in de lottery.

Bone Squash: Yes, and I've come to draw out your affections. Say, you hab me quick, for I 'spect ere long I hab to emigrate furder south. [*Points down.*]

Pompey: Bone Squash, and my darter Junietta, listen to what I exclose. Take her for your oder half, lub her as de possum do de old coon! Neber cross each other in de path ob felicitous domestications, as Jonas dat build de Ark say, de debil be sure to hab you. [*Music, 3 bars. Slaps* Bone Squash *on the back, which makes him start and tremble.*] Why, what's de matter wid de damn'd Nigger. Is he got de shakes?

Bone Squash: I don't like to hear you talk about de debil.

Junietta: Dat's right, neber talk about people you hab not de pleasure of dar acquaintance.

Pompey: Well, well, drop de subject. Mr. Squash, did you 'vite de company?

Bone Squash: Yes, and dey all gwan to Jim Brown's, and den dey all be here. [*Music piano.*] Ah, here dey come.

[*Enter* Jim Brown *with his fiddle.* Amos, Caesar, Mose, Juba, Janza, Milly, *and other blacks. The characters advance to the front, and begin the chorus. During the symphony, they all dance.* Pompey, Junietta, *and* Bone *are on* R.]

Chorus

Come, saw upon de fiddle now,

Old Jim Brown.

[*Repeat, three times*]

Till we cut de pigeon wing,

And hab a break down.

Come, pull out your rosin now,
And grease up your strings.
[*Repeat*]
Bone Squash, take de lead,
And we all will begin.
Dance
We don't fear de constable,
No, by gosh!
[*Repeat, three times*]
While we dance at de wedding,
Ob old Bone Squash.
Strike upon de tambourine
And upon de fiddle, too.
Oh, neber mind de Nigger,
If he habn't got de shoe.

[*Dance, as before. The following is the order of dance.* Amos *advances with* Janza *and* Milly, *who dance to* Mose, *etc. The others dance without precision, following down to lights, to begin chorus.*]

Bone Squash: Gemmen, I 'blige to all ob you! 'Low me to introduce to you Mrs. Squash, my wife dat is to be.

Jim Brown: Mr. Squash, I rader tink de last chimney you swept, you bring down de deposits. [*All laugh.*]

Caesar: I guess he come down de wrong chimney, when de gemmen was down to breakfast. [*All laugh.*]

Bone Squash: Why, look here, gemmen: did you neber see one ob de aristocracy before? [*All laugh.*] Gemmen, de ladies will expire to get ready for de wedd'n. [*Music. Exeunt* Pompey *and ladies.*]

Caesar: But, Mr. Squash, tell us how you come so rich.

[*Music. Solo*]

Bone Squash:

> It was de oder morning,
> About de break ob day,
> As I was gwan up Broadway
> I see'd de high prize
> In de window for sale,
> I went in and paid my money on the nail.
>
> Dis mornin' I found,
> To my great surprise,
> De ticket what I buy'd,
> Drew de big high prize.
>
> I went to de tailors,
> And buy'd der clothes,
> Paid my money like a white man,
> And off I goes.
> [*Chorus.*]
> Pompey Duckellegs, he see'd me,
> And took me by de hand,
> And says, "I want a son-in-law,
> And you is de man.
> You hab got fine clothes,
> And de cash beside,
> My daughter Junietta,
> Shall be your bride."

After chorus, re-enter Pompey, Junietta, *and all the ladies.*

Bone Squash: Now, let de ceremony proceed. [*Music. A chord.*]

Enter Spruce Pink, L.

Spruce: Stop dem perjured nuptializations.

[*Ladies scream—Gentlemen support them.*]

   Bone Squash: Who is dis Nigger?
   Spruce: I am the victim of despair.
   Junietta: Oh, can I believe my eyes! It is—
   Mose: Spruce Pink, what cut my 'quaintance this morning.
   Caesar: You ought to see him cut, when de constable is comin'.
   Spruce: Oh, you am Caesar, de Nigger who run de wheelbarrow ober me dis mornin'. Now, my satisfaction calls for revenge.

[*Music.* Spruce *draws his sword cane. A general scream, when the* Devil *appears up trap. Gong and hurried music, blue lights, etc.*]

   All: The devil! The devil!

[*All stand shaking with fear. Music for the* Devil *to step, increasing to forte every minute.*]

   Devil: Bone Squash, what do you say to emigrating?
   Bone Squash: I can't go jist yet. I am gwan to be married.
   Devil: So much the better; bring your wife along. [Junietta, *at the word "wife," gets behind her father.*] Won't you come?
   Bone Squash: No.
   Devil: Then I'll bring you.

[*Music. As the* Devil *raises his fork, the characters scream, and run to* L. *General commotion, men tripping and rolling over each other.* Bone *gets behind the* Devil—*breaks through all. When, in confusion, the* Devil, *tumbles into basket, the lobster catches hold of his nose—he roars violently.* Bone *escapes up the chimney. All exit, while* Pompey *beats the* Devil *with a broom stick. Red fire used in the chimney, trap, and wings. Curtain.*]

➻❮

Act 2

Scene 1.[16] *A street, as before*

Enter Spruce Pink *meeting* Jim Brown.

Spruce: How are you after your horrification?

Jim Brown: I don't mind de disappointment of de wedding, nor de debil grabbing Bone Squash, but, my fiddle! Look at my fiddle—de notes of mine no longer vibrate on mine ear. All gone to de debil, along wid Bone Squash.

Spruce: And dat Miss Duckellegs, too. If you believe me, I stand four hours in de sun wid her yesterday—and now to resignate me for a patent sweeper!

Jim Brown: I thought de Nigger didn't buy dem clothes honest. He said he draw a prize in de lottery.

Spruce: I think de debil got a prize now.

Enter Bone Squash.

Bone Squash: Look here Niggers where de debil is—

Exit Spruce *and* Brown

Bone Squash: Whew! De Niggers run away from me as if I was de Cogeramorbus. I wonder whar Missus Squash, dat what to be, is? I guess she kind ob alter her notion now. Well, I is de nastiest looking Nigger I eber did see. I kind ob tink my closhes want brushing. Well, dat's de last chimney I sweep for noting. I don't know whar de debil went, but I spect he cut after some other Nigger, jist to pay the expenses. Eh! Eh! Ah, who is dis come dar? Dat's my old sweetheart Janza Snowball. I jist lay back and sight de movements.

[*Retires* L.H.]

Enter Janza

Janza: Well I'm glad de debil is got 'em. What he gwan to be married to old Pompey Duckelleg's daughter, when he tells me he lub me better den a johnny cake.

Bone Squash: But I'm afraid dat johnny cake is dough.

Janza: Who's dere? Mr. Squash! Why, I tought de debil had you.

Bone Squash: Oh, no. He made a mistake, you see. He came arter anoder Nigger whose name was—

Janza: Spruce Pink.

Bone Squash: Oh, dat's his name! But he could not tink of it, so he axed for Bone Squash and Spruce Pink. Bone Squash sound bery much alike. Bone Squash, especially.

Janza: Den, Mr. Squash, I presume all my lub and fections for you.

Bone Squash: Den let's get married right off.

Business[17]

Enter Junietta.

Junietta: What, Bone Squash came back again?

Bone Squash: Oh, de debil.

Janza: Run, Squash, here comes de oder one.

Business

Junietta: Upon my word, Mr. Squash I tought was in de oder world, when to my stonishment I cotch him right before de door making lub to anoder Lady [*aside*]. Tis well for you, Mr. Squash, I hab neber seen such vulgar things. Oh, I neber shall hab de fortitude to hold you.

Bone Squash: If you only hab patience, I'll marry both ob you.

Song

When two evils am to choose,
Dey say take de least one.
If I gib my hand here,
De oder will be undone.
What shall I do
To get me out dis mess?

> Either way I turn,
> My bosom all on fire.
> Ladies, dry your grief,
> And wipe away your sorrow,
> And if you mind's your eye,
> I'll marry you both tomorrow.
>
> *Exeunt*

→←

Scene 2. Cellar in the Five Points. Bar, with liquor for sale—hogsheads. All discovered. As curtain rises, a general laugh.

Jim Brown: I wonder where Mr. Squash is by dis time? Hallo!

> *Enter* Bone Squash, C. *door. Music.*

Bone Squash: Here I am, Niggers! [*Solo—music*] "Look at my dandy coat." Come Niggers, I'll stand a treat, and den I'll tell you whar I've been. [*Goes to bar*]

Spruce [*aside*]: Mr. Bone Squash am now a-going it among de Niggers. I take de 'wantage ob his absence, and go hab an explanation wid Miss Duckellegs. Oh! de perfidious woman ob her sex. [*Exit, L.H.*]

Amos: Mr. Bone, guess you've been leaning against a coal yard.

Bone Squash: Oh, leff off your fun, and I'll tell you all about it.

> Music—Solo and Chorus.

Bone Squash:

> In a chimney tight,
>   I staid all night,
> And like to die,
>   Wid de soot and smoke.
> While de fire below,
>   It burn my toe,

And wid de cinders,
  Like to choke.

Chorus:

> And sich a gittin' up stairs
> And a runnin' from de debil
> Sich a gittin' up stairs,
> I neber did see.

Bone Squash:

Old Pompey Duckellegs
  Turn'd blue,
And shouted out,
  Young hally loo!
De daughter, she
  Was left alone,
And de oder ladies
  Scampered home.

Chorus:

> And sich a gittin' up stairs, etc.

Bone Squash:

Come now, I'll stand,
  Anoder treat,
And at de ball,
  Dis night we'll meet.
And if de debil
  Should creep in,
De way we'll use him,
  Be a sin.

Chorus:

> And sich a gittin' up stairs, etc.
> [*All retire to drink.* Brown *and* Mose *remain in front.*]

Jim Brown: I say, Mose, let us play a game ob luck.

Mose: I've got no money.

Jim Brown: Mr. Squash has, and I'll get de loaded dice.

Mose: Well, you rope him in, and I'll gib you de items.

Jim Brown: Gemman! Let's play, to see who shall hab de most money.

Bone Squash: I've got de most already; but, come, I'm agreed.

[*Music.* Mose *brings a table to C., over the trap.* All *shake their boxes.*]

Solo and Chorus

Smile my fortune!
  Oh, oh, oh!
I'll play you for a dollar, boys.
  I'm as good as you.
And I'll win all your money, boys.
  Ha! ha! ha!
And I'll win all your money, boys.
  Ha! ha! ha!

Hear de chinkling
  Oh, oh, oh!
And de merry clinkling,
  Oh, oh, oh!
Here goes for raffle sixes,
  Worse den before.
I'll double down de money, boys,
  Ha! ha! ha!
I'll double down de money, boys,
  Ha! ha! ha!

Smile my fortune!
  Oh, oh, oh!

Smile my fortune!
    Oh, oh, oh!
I'll sweep it like a hawk, now,
    Twelve! Eh, eh!
Wake snakes, and talk now,
    Three, two, one!
Oh, you'll win all my money, boys!
    Ha! ha! ha!

Smile my fortune!
    Oh, oh, oh!
Smile my fortune!
    Oh, oh, oh!
I'll go you all my money, now,
    Make de pile large!
I'll go you all my money, now,
    Make de pile large!
Now, show your black faces once,
    Six! no more!
Only show your black faces, now,
    Worse den before.

I've lost my fortune!
    Oh, oh, oh!
I've lost my fortune!
    Oh, oh, oh!
So gib me back my money, boys,
    Ha! ha! ha!
Oh, gib me back my money, boys,
    Ha! ha! ha!
I wish de debil had me,
    Ha! ha! ha!

I wish de debil had me,
Ha! ha! ha!
[*Hurried music.*]
Enter Devil *through the table.*

All: Oh, debil! He's come.

All thrown into confusion. The Devil *leaps from the table, and the characters run out. As* Bone Squash *is about to follow, the* Devil *stops him with his fork.*

Devil: Oh, you damn Nigger; I've got you now.
Bone Squash: Well, I rader tink you'll hab to run for it.

[*Music.*]

[*As* Bone *is making again for the door, enter all the characters. The* Devil *seizes one part of* Bone's *coat tail; the blacks being divided, one half seize the* Devil's *tail, and the other half the tail of* Bone. *They struggle violently, when* Bone's *coat tears up the back.* Bone *escapes through the door in flat, leaving his coat tail behind. The characters all tumble. The* Devil *makes after* Bone, *the rest following.*]

All: Go it, Bone!

➤◄

Scene 3. Exterior of Barber's shop, with a large window to break. Enter Bone *and* Devil, *R.H. The* Devil *tries in vain to throw a rope over* Bone's *head.* Bone, *seeing no other hope left, plunges through the window, the* Devil *after him.* [*Change. Music continued.*]

➤◄

Scene 4. Interior of Barber's shop, in horrible confusion. Bone *is discovered with half his body out of window. The* Devil *has hold of him by the leg. In the other window, the others are thronged, anxiously viewing the scene.*

Devil: I've got you now like an oyster has a crab, right by the leg.

Bone Squash: Oh, look here, Mr. Yankee debil, stop! I splain the matter!

Devil: Well, gab you, it's nearly dinner time. You call yourself a business man, do you? Why, they'd kick you out of the Exchange, even on Sunday. Why, curse your color, you aren't fit to sell second-hand coffins. You're like a sand clam commission merchant: you'd walk two miles for one, for fear of meeting your creditors.

Bone Squash: Well, look here, look here, who told you to come to de wedding widout de inbertation, and make me pear so diclous 'fore the ladies?

Devil: Well, I rather calculate we didn't say anything about the time. I guess it's optional.

Bone Squash [*aside*]: Dars where he hab me. But look here, Mr. Debil, I believe I shall take de benefit ob de act.[18]

Devil: Oh, get out, only hearken to your gab. Come now, act white, if you are black.

Jim Brown: Bone, put out!

Devil: No, you don't.

[*Music.* Bone *attempts to run, but is tripped up by a noose the* Devil *has fixed to his leg while talking to him. All laugh.*]

Bone Squash: Who tied that rope round my leg?

Devil: I wanted to pull the kinks out. Why, you fire knot chunk, you're like a 'lasses candy in a shop window. You run away all sides. Come, I think we'd better go. The people will be coming out of church, and I don't want to be mobb'd in the street. They're keeping up a milliner's birthday and I'll make sure of you this time.

Winds his tail round him

Jim Brown: Bone, sham sick!

Bone Squash: Oh! Mr Debil, I tink I got de measles.

Devil: Well, here's an antidote. [*Music. Devil takes out a long cigar, and begins to smoke it. He lights it from a phosphorus box in his tail.*] Do you smoke?

Bone Squash: No, I tank you. I'm free from all sich wulgar wices. Eh! What a pain I've got in my leg. Oh! Oh! Oh!

Devil: Why, how you talk! Come along with me, and I'll give you a sulphur bath.

Jim Brown: It's all day wid him.

Mose: Squash, is you gwan to take your brush wid you?

Caesar: Mr. Squash, any word to send to Mrs. Squash dat was to be?

Bone Squash: Look here, jist gib me time to speak to my feller citizens.

Devil: Oh, come now; you're like a rent day, no getting you off.

Bone Squash: Well, if I must, I must. Eh! eh!

Music—Solo and Chorus

Bone Squash:

> Listen while I splain de matter,
> Bout my lub, sweet Junietta. [*A start*]
> Tomorrow we gwan to marry.
> And you no longer leff me tarry. [*Start*]
> And I gib my word and honor,
> To meet you on de Five Points corner,
> And go straight along wid you,
> And go straight along wid you,
> But at present must excuse me,
> And tomorrow you may use me
> And tomorrow, and tomorrow,
> Please to leff me stay.

Devil:

> No, I must haste away.

Bone Squash:

> Pray excuse me.

All:

> Ha! ha! ha!

Devil:

> I must use you.

Bone Squash:

> Please let me stay.

All:

> Ha! ha! ha!

Devil:

> I must away.

All:

> Ha! ha! ha!

Bone Squash:

> Farewell all my calculation.[19]
> For I'm bound to de wild goose station. [*Start*]
> Farewell, all your fancy balls.
>> [*Start.* Brown *gives knife.*]
> Yes, I must confess my sorrow.
> Since I cannot stay tomorrow.
> Farewell all, Bone Squash is gone,
> If you only would excuse me,
> And tomorrow you may use me,
> And tomorrow, and tomorrow,
> So please to leff me stay.
>> [*Chorus as before*]

All: Cut! cut!

[Bone *cuts the* Devil's *tail off and escapes. All finish chorus.* Devil *pursues* Bone, *the others following.*]

→←

Scene 5.[20] *A Street. Music. Enter* Bone *and all the ladies,* L.H.
                                   Song and Chorus.
Bone Squash:

> Oh, ladies, pray, don't tease me so,
> But please to let me go;
> Heigho! my pretty gals,
> Please to let me go.

Ladies [*first chorus*]:

> You shall not go!
> You shall not go!

Bone Squash:

> Heigho! my pretty gals,
> Do let me go.

Ladies [*second chorus*]:

> Heigho! My pretty Bone
> You shall not go.

Bone Squash:

> I'm a gwan to Philadelphy,
> Whar I will be safe, I know.
>
>   *First Chorus.*

Bone Squash:

> I've just escaped de constable,
> Who'd got me safe in tow.
>
>   *Second Chorus.*

Bone Squash:

> If you keep me here, my Johnny-cake
> Will all be turned to dough.
>
>   *First Chorus.*

Bone Squash:

> I must break dis link ob harmony,
> And trust to heel and toe.
>> *Second Chorus.*

Bone Squash:

> Let go your hands, and let me troop
> I'm anxious for to go.
>> *First Chorus.*

Bone Squash:

> If you eber showed compassion,
> Now's the time to let it flow.
>> *Second Chorus.*

> [*Exit* Bone, *pulling the girls after him.*]

>←

Scene 6. The whole stage. A balloon ready for ascending. Two little devils filling it with bellows. All the characters discovered on each side the stage for the finale. Music.

> *Enter* Bone Squash, *crazy.*

Bone Squash:

> Save me! save me! save me!

Omnes:

> Oh, what is de matter now
> Wid old Bone Squash? [*Repeat.*]

Bone Squash:

> Save me! save me! save me!

Men:

> Oh! oh! oh!

Bone Squash:

> Sorry dat I sold myself to de Debil.

Omnes:

Sorry dat he sold himself to de Debil.

Women:

Poor Bone Squash!

Bone Squash:

Oh! oh! oh!

Omnes:

Poor Bone Squash!

Bone Squash:

Juny! Juny! Fare you well for ever!

Omnes:

Oh! oh! oh!

Bone Squash:

What dis I see?

Women:

Junietta, lubly dear.

Bone Squash:

What dis I see?

Men:

You promised marriage here.

Bone Squash:

Go whar I will.

Women:

Go whar you will.

Bone Squash:

Spruce Pink can't come here,
He's gone below.

Men:

He's gone below.

Bone Squash:

Tremble and fear.

Women:

                Tremble and fear.

Omnes:

                Oh! oh! oh!

                Tremble and fear.

Bone Squash:

    And I scamper down the street,

    Ebry Nigger dat I meet,

    And I ups wid a penny,

    Head or tail for a treat.

Omnes:

    And he scampers down the street,

    Ebry Nigger dat he meets,

    He ups wid a penny,

    Head or tail for a treat.

Bone Squash:

    Save me! save me! save me!

Men:

    Carry him along! Carry him along!

Bone Squash:

    Save me! save me! save me!

Men:

    Carry him along! Carry him along!

Bone Squash:

    Save me! save me! save me!

Women:

                Poor Bone Squash!

Men:

                Oh! oh! oh!

Bone Squash:

                Sich a gittin' up stairs

                And a runnin' from de debil

Sich a gittin' up stairs,
I neber did see.

Omnes:

Sich a gittin' up stairs
And a runnin' from de debil
Sich a gittin' up stairs,
We neber did see.

Bone Squash:

Ladies, dry your grief,
And wipe away your sorrow,
And if you mind's your eye,
I'll marry you all tomorrow.

Omnes:

Oh, de Nigger must be crazy,
It's bery plain to see;
De Debil's comin' after him,
He can't get free.

Bone Squash:

When I fust left Kentucky,—

Women:

With sorrow he grieves for his home.

Bone Squash:

My heart filled with joy was too happy.

Men:

Like de smoke from the chimney is blown.

Bone Squash:

Den fill de cup,
And leff me sup,
Dar's nothing like good whiskey,
I've fled de track
And can't come back,
Darfore I will be frisky.

Omnes:

> Den fill de cup,
> And leff him sup,
> Dar's nothing like good whiskey,
> He's fled de track
> And can't come back,
> Darfore we will be frisky.

Bone Squash:

> Smile my fortune!

Men:

> Oh! oh! oh!

Bone Squash:

> Smile my fortune!

Men:

> Oh! oh! oh!

Bone Squash:

And I've lost all my money, boy.

Omnes:

Ha! ha! ha!

Bone Squash:

> Here goes for raffle sixes,

Omnes:

> Ha! ha! ha!

Bone Squash:

> Here goes for raffle sixes,

Omnes:

> Ha! ha! ha!

Bone Squash:

> Oh! oh! oh!
> It is my Junietta's voice.

Omnes:

> Ha! ha! ha!

Bone Squash:

    Oh, ladies do not tease me so,

    But please to let me go.

Omnes:

        Heigho! my boy Squash,

        Indeed, you shall not go.

Women:

        You shall not go!

Omnes:

        Heigho! my pretty Squash,

        You shall not go.

Bone Squash:

        It's too late to repent of my folly now;

        It's too late to repent of my folly now!

Omnes:

           The Debil will hab him,

           He's sure for to grab him.

           And away goes Bone Squash to—

Bone Squash:

        Fill de cup,

        And leff me sup,

    Dar's nothing like good whiskey,

        I've fled de track

        And can't come back,

    Darfore I will be frisky.

Omnes:

        Come fill de cup

        And leff him sup

    Dar's nothing like good whiskey,

        He's fled de track

        And can't come back,

    Darfore we will be frisky.

Bone Squash:

    Come on! Come on!

    Dar's nought can save me,

    De Debil, he's sure to hab me.

    None to pity dis poor Nigger;

    He will hab to groan for eber. [*Gong.*]

    Save me! Save me! Save Me!

Omnes:

    Ha! ha! ha!

[*Enter the* Devil *with torch and a bundle of straw. He seizes* Bone Squash, *and puts him in car of balloon. Balloon ascends, surrounded with Fireworks.* Bone *cuts the rope; the* Devil *falls and* Bone *ascends, throwing out his shoes, hat, etc. The* Devil *falls through a trap, and red fire is emitted from the same. Curtain falls on tableau.*]

The End

Otello

A Burlesque Opera[1]

Act 1

Scene 1. Stage ¼ dark. Front Street, House in L. H. *Flat:*
Window and Door used: knocker on door. Enter Roderigo *and* Iago,
R.H.

> Roderigo

Pshaw that's all gammon,[2] and what makes it worse,
You know you always could command my purse
As if the strings were thine—[*aside*] when it was empty—
Yet would not that to honest friendship tempt ye?

> Iago

Well, how you talk. Say, did I ever spare him?

> Roderigo

Didn't you tell me that you couldn't bear him?

> Iago

Well, no more; I can't and I've good cause to hate.
I'll tell you how he "sarved me out" of late.
Three great men of the City—aye and wise men—
To make me one of Venice's Excisemen
Tried all their interest and walked some miles
From one to t'other, even doffed their tiles
To this same nigger—who said he do his best
But in dat department he hab no interest;

He did not like in piping times of peace
To urge upon de Town a "new police."
But if the common council next election "hatch,"
He'd make me Captain of the City Watch—
You go de ticket, de council dey will pay
And raise de salary, quarter dollar a day.³
The Aldermen did all their pledges fill
But curse the Mayor—he vetoed the bill.
He saw my friends were hurt and so, says he,
If he'll serve in de army under me,
I'll make him Ensign. So the post I've got—
But twixt ourselves, I don't like being shot.

   Roderigo

Then why d'ye follow him?

   Iago

                              You just lay low.
I'll some day kick up such a precious row.
I'll seem to be his most particular friend
And thus more easily will gain my end.
I've plenty of stout friends about the Man—
We'll kick him—if we can but git him down.
The gal . . .

   Roderigo

   A lucky nigger is this thick-lip chap.

   Iago

Let's call her Daddy who's taking his first nap.

   Roderigo

[*Crosses to left*] I'll call him up. [*knocks*]

   Iago

   Don't knock so loud
Or else about the house you'll get a crowd.

Music—"Merry Swiss Boy"[4]
Roderigo
Come arouse thee; arouse thee, Brabantio arise!
And look to your daughter and your bags.

Iago
What ho, there Brabantio, Old Signor arise!
Or you'll not have a stiver[5] or a rag.
There's thieves on the premises, so look to your life—
Your daughter's squatulated[6] and become a nigger's wife.

Both
Come arouse thee, arouse thee, Brabantio arise
And look to your daughter and your bags.

Brabantio appears at window with blunderbuss

Brabantio
What's the reason of this rumpus,
And this knocking at my door,
When honest folks should all be in bed?

Iago
You are robbed, Sir—oh, your daughter
With the Moor has run away.

Roderigo
It's a fact, Sir, indeed what we've said.

Brabantio
I know thee, Roderigo.
And I've told thee off before:
Never let me catch you loafing
Round about my door.

Roderigo and Iago
We beseech you—we beseech you,
Straight satisfy yourself,
If she be in her chamber
Or her house.

Brabantio

Get me lights and get me tapers

Till I satisfy myself

If she be in her chamber

Or the house.

   [Dialogue]

   Brabantio

Holla there, who is making such a clatter?

Who are you? What the devil is the matter?

   Roderigo

Why, you've been robbed—oh! Could I have caught her!

A nigger's just now bolted with your daughter.

   Brabantio

The trick won't do—I know it's all my eye.

I don't believe a word on't. It's a lie.

You think to have her for yourself—but won't.

You want my daughter.

   Roderigo

                                        On my life, I don't.

   Brabantio

Should there be truth in this—I'm in a fright.

I'll get the tinder box and strike a light.

                                        exit from window

                    Iago [*sings*]

Farewell, friend Roddy, I'll now cut my stick.[7]

Rather than meet Brabantio, I'd meet Old Nick.[8]

Who knows but what he'd take it in his noddle,

And straight before the Duke to make me toddle—

There to confront and give my testimony

Against Otello and fair Desdemona.

The state, I know, cannot do without him,

So I rather guess I'll not say much about him,
And though I hate him as I hate the devil,
I'd cut his throat but wouldn't be uncivil.[9]

Exit R. H.

[*Lights up*] *Enter* Brabantio *and all the servants from door in flat*
    Brabantio
There's no mistake, the nigger's back I'll fleece.[10]
Give notice, do, good Sir—to the Police.
    Roderigo
Notice alone will but the case retard,
Unless you offer, too, a good reward.
    Brabantio
D'ye think they're married? Where were they seen?
    Roderigo
Last on their road, he told, to Gretna Green.[11]
    Brabantio
Rascals bestir ye! Try to overtake her
Before this nigger chap his wife can make her.
        The two go off L. H. *(Music until off)*[12]
Sirrahs, go: some of you, call up my brother,
Some one way—some the other.
On, good Roderigo, I'll deserve your pains
When we do catch her, then count your gains.

Exeunt L. H.

➜←

Scene 2. Another Street. (Lights up) Enter Iago *and* Otello, R. H.
    Iago
Though often in a row I've knocked down men
And, had I causes, would do the same again,
But, cut a throat? I rather guess I'm nervous—

For I lack villains to do me service.

Nine or ten times my passion so high rose

I thought to have given him a bloody nose . . .

    Otello

All better as it is—

    Iago

                But his tongue went—

    Otello

Let him do his spite,

De sarbices dat I hab done, will set me right.

You know, Iago, as you my crony,

I dearly lub de gentle Desdemony.

But see what lights am dem what's coming yonder?

    Iago

It is her daddy, looking black as thunder!

It's true your courage never had a doubt,

He's in a rage—you'd better, Sir, put out.

    Otello

What? Cut my stick? Dat, you mean to say?

Dis child's Otello—sogers don't run away.

Enter Brabantio *and* four attendants *with lights,* Roderigo *and* two
                    policemen

    Brabantio (dress disordered)

There, that's the nigger—Seize him I command.

    Iago

You, Roderigo, come, Sir—hand to hand.

                    They draw swords; policemen seize Otello

    Otello

You want my purse?

    1st Policeman

             Oh, certainly for that . . .

2nd Policeman

Don't hold the gentlemen so hard, you Pat . . .

Roderigo

You're summoned to the Council of the Nation.

Brabantio

Pshaw, nonsense, off with him to the station.

He's ruined my daughter. He shall rue it.

Otello gives purse to policeman[13]

1st Policeman

We can't take him—cause we didn't see him do it.

Enter Cassio L. H.

Cassio

Faith, you're a nice man, ain't you? By the powers,

You've kept the Senate waiting [*looking at watch*] just two
   hours.

Otello

Twasn't my fault, I would not, Sir, hab tarried,

But for my farder-in-law.

Brabantio

        Damn 'em, then they are married.

Take him in custody. Gentlemen, I insist.

Down with the nigger, if he do resist.

As attendants approach to seize Otello

Music (Three chords)

Otello

Recitative

Hold your hands, all you ob my opinion and de oder ones. Whar it
   my cue to raise a row, I should hab know it widout your telling
   me. And old Massa Signor, you should more command with
   years den with your swordesses. What is you want me for to go
   to answer dis are charges? Nay—to prison.

All exclaim

Aye to prison. [*pointing off*]

Solo and Chorus

What if I do obey you, Sar,
And go along with you?
De duke may be offended
And dis conduct you may rue.
His messengers are here upon
Some business of de state
   And he may be damn angry
     For troubling him so late. [*repeat two last lines*]

Brabantio [*Second Verse*]

The Duke I hear's in Council now
And will be all the night;
And if a white man's justice
The Duke will set me right.
Mine's not a soaplock[14] rowdy spree
That I do want relief.
   But I have lost my daughter, Sir,
     And this chap is the thief. [*repeat two last lines*]

Third Grand Chorus

Come march, Sir, to the Senate
And perhaps you'll there find bail.
Your black looks and your blustering
Will be of no avail.
For if a black shall wed a white,
And afterwards go free,
   In a very pretty pickle then
     Our daughters soon will be. [*repeat two last lines*][15]

Exeunt R. H.

✦

Scene 3. The Senate Chamber. Duke and Senators discovered sitting.
Music "Sitting on a Rail"[16]
Chorus

For council we have met to night,
Like men, to do the thing that's right
And beat the foe that's now in sight.
For Venice shall be free,
Venice shall be free,
Venice shall be free.
We'll beat the foe that's now in sight,
For Venice shall be free.

Music while Brabantio, Otello, Cassio, Iago *and* Roderigo *enter*
Duke

Valiant Otello, we're very glad you've come,
For in this war we fear we'll suffer some.
Would you believe, Sirs—the galley slaves[17]
Are kicking up a dust upon the waves.
Here's one good gentleman, defend us Heaven,
Says there's a hundred and twenty seven.
And, this, my letter, says the slaves that naughty
Amount to full one hundred forty.
The other gentleman has got a letter
Which says two hundred and something better.
What's to be done? Otello: try and lick 'em.
Take all our soldiers and you're sure to nick 'em
Haste them away and do just as you oughter.

Brabantio, rising

Stop, good Sir Duke—he's stole away my daughter.
He is a buzzard.[18] Sir, a very Elf.

I do believe he is the Devil himself.
He has dissolved my daughter into air
Or else has mesmerized her, Heaven knows where.
A rogue—a vagabond—I could his claret spill:[19]
Commit him, I beseech you, to the treading mill.[20]
Oh, that I had him out in Carolino,
I'd tie him up and give him thirty-nino.[21]

   Duke

There must be some mistake. Come speak, Otello.
What say you to the charge, my noble fellow?

   Otello

[*Recitative*[22]] Most potent, grabe, and reberand Signiors, my bery
   noble and approbed good Massas: Dat I hab tuck away dis old
   man's darter—is true and no mistake.[23] True, I's married her. De
   bery head and tail ob my offence hab dis extent, no more: rude
   am I in talk. I cannot chat like some folks for, since a piccanniny
   two years old, I'b always been in rows and spreezes. Yet, by your
   gracious patience, I'll tell you how I won his darter.

   All

Hear him! Hear him! Hear him!

   Duke

Silence. Say it, Otello.

                    Music—Air: "Ginger Blue"[24]
         Her farder lub'd me well
         And he say to me one day,
         Otello, Won't you come wid me and dine?
         As I whar rader sharp set,
         Why, bery well, I say,
         I'll be up to de trough, Sar, in time.
         We had terrapins, chicken stew,
         and nice punking pie,

And a dish filled with nice macaroni,
And last, not least, come de fried sassengers,
All cooked by de fair Desdemona.

2nd Verse

When de dinner it was ober,
And de whiskey flew about,
And de old Man was high in his glory,
He axed me to sing a song,
Fore the company put out.
Or else, would I tell again my story
Ob de sprees dat I get in
And de scrapes dat I get out
And how often run away when leff loose
And how dat I got free
From de Southern Slabery[25]
And how often was I in de Calaboose.[26]

3rd Verse

Now, dese tings to hear,
Desdemona cocked her ear
And wish Heaben hab made
Her sich a nigger.
But den de house affairs
Would call her down stairs
War she'd sit in de corner,
Cry, and snigger.
My story being done,
She only wished I had a son,[27]
And to tell this story
I would undo her.
Den she wink and blink at me—
And I did de same to she.
And upon dis suit, Sar, I won her.

   Brabantio

Tis all a lie, told to defraud the bench.

Please you, order some one fetch the wench

That she may here confront him face to face.

   Otello

Ancient, conduct her, bring her—you best know de place.

                          Exeunt Iago *and* Roderigo L. H.

   Brabantio

And if she do confess she first began

To throw sheep eyes and ogle at the man;

If, as he says, she took these means to woo him—

Then blow me tight if I don't give her to him.

            Enter Desdemona *and* Ladies, Iago *and* Roderigo

Oh here she is—my child—my darling child,

Your poor old father has been almost wild.

But tell me—since you lost your poor dear mother,

Don't you love me dear more than any other?

   Desdemona

Why, my dear father—if I must be candid,

You've loved your child as much as ever man did.

And, as in duty bound, I loved or, rather,

Worshipped my parent. But then you're my father.

I've followed the example of my mother,

Who loved her father but left him for another.

   Brabantio

Madam, your mother never left her home.

   Desdemona

Pshaw, pshaw—confess the case now, do, Sir, do.

Did she not give up all the world for you?

And of her peculation ne'er did rue.

I've only done as folks have done before.

I've cut you all for this—my Blackamoor. [*crosses to Otello*]
He is my husband. What's done can't be undone.

    Otello

Dat am a fact: one and one make one.

Air—"Down Fly Market"[28]

Desdemona

I'll tell you why I loved the Black.

Chorus

Tell us freely—tell us freely!

Desdemona

Every night I had a knack

Chorus

Speak sincerely—speak sincerely!

Desdemona

Of listening to his tales bewitching.

Chorus

Drive us frantic—drive us frantic!

Desdemona

My hair while curling in the kitchen,

Chorus

How romantic—how romantic . . .

2nd Verse

Desdemona

Once while darning father's stocking,

Chorus

Recreation—recreation . . .

Desdemona

Oh, he told a tale so shocking,

Chorus

Execration—execration!

Desdemona

So romantic, yet so tender,

Chorus

Shrewd and witty—shrewd and witty . . .

Desdemona

That I fell across the fender.

Chorus

What a pity, what a pity . . .

3rd Verse

Desdemona

When I came about—ah, me!

Chorus

Rather supple—rather supple . . .

Desdemona

I was sitting on his knee—

Chorus

Loving couple—loving couple!

Desdemona

Greatful for the scrape I'd missed.[29]

Chorus

Tender touches—tender touches!

The Moral

Desdemona

Listen, ladies, if you please,

Chorus

All attention—all attention . . .

Desdemona, rather slower

Never sit on young men's knees,

Chorus

Pray don't mention—pray don't mention!

Desdemona

For though I got a husband by it,

Chorus

Lucky creature—lucky creature!

Desdemona

The plan's not good—so pray don't try it [*goes to Otello*]

Chorus

We beseech you—we beseech you.

Brabantio [*spoken*]

A white man's daughter and a black man's son
Well, Heaven be with you both—for I have done.
A word, Otello: watch her, mind you do—
She cheated me, you know, and may cheat you. [*goes up
    and sits*]

Otello

My life, upon her faith, dar's no mistake.
She only cheated you for her Otello's sake.

Duke

Now then, Otello, that affair's all right—
And you must lumber off this very night.

Otello

Tonight? good Massa, Duke—me[30] just now married.

Duke

I can't help it—go you must—too long you've tarried.
I shall be robbed and murdered by these chaps
If you don't go and whip em for me, p'haps.

Otello

Whar shall I leave my wife?

Desdemona

                          Did you say—leave me?
Do you begin already to deceive me?

Duke

Go to your father, dear.

Desdemona

                    I sha'nt.

Duke

O, fie.

Otello

I won't hab it so.

Brabantio

Nor I.

Desdemona

I won't go anywhere but with Otello.

That's what I want.

Brabantio

Well, don't begin to bellow.

Desdemona

I will—I'll cry for ever—all my life.

What was the use of being made a wife?

Otello

Your voices, fellow citizens, I pray.

Duke

That's a brave lass, and so you shall, I say.

Otello

Honest Iago—you am a cleber fellow.

My wife I leab wid you—Missus Otello.

If she catch cold and gits the cough and sneezes,

Gib her some candy, what you buy at Pease's.

And when she hab packed up her trunks, my man,

Den bring her arter me best way you can.

I'be but an hour, or someting dar about,

To pass wid dee before I do put out.

Duke

Signor, your son, though black as Fancy Rooks,

Is like a singed cat—better than he looks.[31]

Air—"Lucy Long"[32]

Otello

Dont weep, sweet Desdemona,
Kase we must part tonight.
I am a sodger, honey,
And my trade it am to fight.
But when de wars am ober,
I'll return to thee, lub, soon,
As a hero and a lubber,
To keep up our honeymoon.

Chorus

Bravo Otello, He's a clever fellow.
One so glorious, will be victorious.

Otello

Don't cry, sweet Desdemony.

Desdemona

Oh, oh, oh, oh, oh, oh, oh!

Otello

Don't fret, sweet Desdemona,

Chorus

Bravo, Bravo Bravissimo,

Otello [*second verse*]

Black folks from sheer vexation
Will grumble at me a few;
And call dis 'malgamation[33]
Well, I don't care *damn* if they do. [*pause*]
If I hab no objection,
What de debil's dat to dem?
You can't help your complexion;
Nature made you as well as dem.

Chorus

Bravo Otello: he's a clever fellow;
One so glorious, will be victorious.

Otello

Don't fret sweet Desdemony.

Desdemona

Oh, oh, oh, oh, oh, oh,

Otello

Don't fret, sweet Desdemony.

Chorus

Bravo, Bravo, Bravissimo.

Desdemona [*third verse*]

Where's the use of getting married
If our husbands have to roam?
Far better to have tarried
A single life at home.
For, if this is a beginning,
I plain 'gin to see,
This thing called matrimony
Is not the thing crack'd up to be.

Chorus

Bravo Otello: he's a clever fellow
One so glorious, will be victorious.

Otello

Don't fret, sweet Desdemony.

Desdemona

Oh, oh, oh, oh, oh, oh,

Otello

Don't fret sweet Desdemony.

Chorus

Bravo, Bravo, Bravissimo.

Exit Otello, Desdemona; Duke *and* attendants, Brabantio *and*
Policemen, L. H.

Business of tossing with Duke and Brabantio

Roderigo

Iago,

   Iago

   What's the matter with the chap?

   Roderigo

I'll drown myself.

   Iago

   Oh, git out, you silly chap.

   Roderigo

Silly, indeed; answer me this query,

Why should I live when done out of my deary?

   Iago

Oh, hush! Shut up your trap—she loves you still.

Or, if she does not, I rather guess she will.

No matter how—it's the fashion nowadays;

If you would win her, sport the rhino.[34] Come,

Put money in your purse—she's yours, by gum.

Drown yourself, eh? Why, what a silly body!

Hark you, go drown care and take an apple toddy.

   Roderigo

It must be so—I'm really tired of thinking,

And blow me tight, if I don't take to drinking.

   Iago

That's the ticket, meet me again tonight—

I'll sarve this black chap out, else I'm not white.

   Duet—"Polly will you now"[35]

   Iago and Roderigo

   Iago

   I have told you oft,

   And I tell you again,

How worse than pisen[36]
I hate the Moor.
For, to my wife,
Upon my life,
He's been making love
To her, I'm sure.
Now, if his wife you once can count,
You'll make him jealous and me a sport.
Put money in your purse.
Put money in your purse,
And that's the way we'll have revenge.
Put money in your purse.

> *Roderigo* [*Second Verse*]

Will you, indeed,
If I succeed
To get the wife
From this black Chap,
Should it come to blows
And a bloody nose,
Stand from behind me,
At my back?
For, by the mass,
Should this pretty lass
Just get a glimpse at me, my boy,
From the highest window
No doubt she'll throw
Herself in the arms of Roderigo!

> *Iago*

Put money in your purse!
Put money in your purse,

And that's the way we'll have revenge.

Put money in your purse.

Exeunt L. H.

>←

Scene 4. Cyprus. Enter Cassio R. H.

    Cassio

Faith, then I wish Otello, safe and sound,

Was treading once again upon the ground.

For while on terra firma all seems level

The sea beyon't is rolling like the devil [*gun fire*]

Sure that's the signal, then he's come at last.

                    Enter Montano L. H.

    Montano

A ship—a ship—has just her anchor cast

And one Iago's come.

    Cassio

               Iago said ye

Then, by the powers, he's brought the Captain's lady.

    Montano

What? Is Otello married? Why, how is this?

    Cassio

And to as fine a gal as one could kiss.

Mistress Iago's come too—for 'tis said,

She's to the bride, a sort of Lady's maid . . . [*laugh* L. H.]

By the hokey's and here they are.

            Enter Desdemona, Emilia, ladies, child[37] *and* Iago, L. H.

    Cassio

Madam, I wish you joy.

Blood an' zouns and whiskey, what a bouncing boy!

Mistress Iago, I'm glad to see you, too.

Mister Iago, Sir, the same to you. [*crosses to* L. C.]

For old acquaintance sake; give us a buss.

Don't mind your husband—he'll not raise a fuss. [*kisses*
   Emilia]

   Iago

Oh, pile on a load or two; don't mind me, pray,

'Stead of her lip—would she'd give her tongue away.

She often blows me up—

   Emilia

              You tell a lie.

I never blow you up, you fool, not I.

Except when you get into brawls and fights,

And come home reeling every hour of the night.

You've killed my peace and almost broke my heart.

Oh, if I had some friend to take my part. [*falls on Cassio's neck*]

Wait 'til I get home! You say I scold you?

I'll make the house, you wretch, too hot to hold you.

   Desdemona

I never hear her scold, nor think she can;

So don't you be so cross, you naughty man.

What would you say of woman, if you could

Find one amongst us that was very good?

           Air—"Yankee Doodle"[38]

        Iago

      I'll tell you. [cue for orchestra]

      Now, she that's fair and never proud,

      A gal so nice and cozy,

      A smartish tongue—but never loud—

      And lips so red and rosy,

      With lots of cash—but none too gay—

      Just neat and not too dashy,

With locks just the flowers of May,
and bonnet not too splashy.

Second Verse

The gal that being in a rage
And could keep down her dander;
One who in scandal won't enquire
Nor go ahead on slander;
One who could think without a word—
Where do you think I'll find her?
One who a young man's footstep heard
And would not look behind her.

[*Spoken*] She'd be the critter that I see very clear.

    Desdemona

For what—

    Iago

 To pickle tripe and bottle ginger beer!

    Desdemona

Your wit and spleen are both surcharged in vapour.
You shan't write puffs for me in Bennett's paper.[39]

    Cassio

Oh, don't you mind or care a fig about him.
Faith, he's a ladies man; the devil doubt him.

                      Takes her hand, both retire up

    Iago

He takes her by the hand and slaps her shoulder,
I'll have you stranger,[40] yet, ere you're much older.

                      Otello sneezes without

The Moor! I swan, I know him by his sneeze.

    Desdemona

Come then we'll go and meet him, if you please.

Music and crash of Symbols [*sic*][41]
Enter Otello *and* attendants, L. H.

Otello

Oh, my fair warrioress, I embrace dee thus!
Welcome, Honey, to de town of Cyprus.

Desdemona

Behold this pledge—your image here is seen.
Not this side love, the other side I mean [*points to child's face*].[42]

Otello *takes the boy and kisses him*

Otello [*to* Cassio]

How do our old acquaintance of the Isle?
Honey, you shall be well-desired de while.

Music—"The Girl I Left Behind Me"[43]

Otello

My wonder's great as my content
To see you here before me,
Because you said, before I went,
You bery much adore me.
If arter tempest comes sich calm,
De winds may blow and find me,
I don't care damn—when in dese arms
De gal I leff behind me.

Second Verse

To die would be most happy now.
I'd kick de bucket freely—
But leab you, lub, a widow now
Would grieb me too sincerely.
May dis our greatest discord be [*embrace*]
And lub still deeper bind me,
Nor grief nor sorrow eber cross
De gal I leff behind me.

Third Verse
I've libed on land; I've libed on sea,
In ebery clime and station.
And dere no station in all de world
Like de state of annexation.
Kase if you like me, and I like you,
And our lubs are in communion,
De longer den de family grows,
More stronger am de Union.

Iago
You're well tuned now. I'll give you sich a kick
I will bring you down a peg and stop your music.

Otello
Now for our honey moon. Our deeds are crowned,
De wars am ended, and de Turks am drowned.
Come, dear, let us in to dinner—
Welcome, once more, to Cyprus or I'm a sinner.

Air—"Nix my Dolly"[44]

Otello
Oh, de wars and de scrapes
And de sprees am done—sprees am done
De foe am beat.
De Turks am drowned—Turks am drowned.
All safe and sound
To our wives we come
Wid de sprigs of laurel
In battle we won.
    Den drink, my boys,
    Dar's notin' to pay. [*repeat*]
    Drink deep, drink deep, 'tis a holly day.

Second Verse
Otello

Once more well met in Cyprus here,
My duck, my lub, my charming dear.
Iago, my coffers you disembark,
And bring de Captain to hab a lark.
　　　Den drink, my boys,
　　　Dar's notin' to pay [*repeat*]
　　　Drink deep, drink deep,
　　　Dar's notin' to pay. [*Music*]

Chorus and dance: exit Otello, Desdemona, Emilia *and* child, R. H.

Iago

Come here, Roderigo, [*Enter* Roderigo L. H.] I've just now
　　seen 'em;
I swan, there's pretty goings on between 'em.

Roderigo

Between 'em—between who?

Iago

　　　　Hush, man, lay low.
Just put your finger thus [*to nose*] and you shall know,
I tell you: Cassio's now her fancy man.
The Black was all a whim. D'ye think she can
Care that [*snaps fingers*] for him, while you or I
Would cast sheep's eyes at her—or heave a sigh?
Wouldn't she take your squeezing notion civil,
Rather than cuddles from the very devil.

Roderigo

I can't believe it, bless her. She's so good!

Iago

Bless'd apple sarce—Ain't sawdust made of wood?

Isn't she, flesh and blood, her mother's darter?
Ain't pancakes made of eggs and flour?

   Roderigo

and water?

   Iago

A bless'd huckleberry pudding then! Hearken to me:
Cassio keeps watch this very night, d'ye see?
Go you and tease him, blow him up or, damn him,
If that won't do, with brandy toddy cram him.

   Roderigo

I'll do it. Dear Iago, where shall we meet?

   Iago

This evening, on the corner of this street.

   Roderigo

I will, adieu. [*exits* L. H.]

   Iago

The same to you.

                Air—"Rosin the Bow"[45]
      That Cassio loves her, I believe it.
      And she loves this Cassio, no doubt,
      But if I once catch 'em together,
      I'll be darned if I don't blab it out.
      Like brimstone, her husband I hate,
      And I'll worry him out of his life,
      For I see by the papers, of late,
      He's been making love, too, to my wife.
             Second Verse
      I'll give Michael Cassio tarnation,
      But not till I first get him drunk.
      And as no law protects reputation,
      I'll swear he's been stealing a trunk.

This vengeance I'll not let it slip,
And to morrow I'll at it right slap,
I'll have Mr. Mike on the hip,
Cause he's also had on my night cap.

Third Verse

I'll make this Otello so jealous,
This pudding he'll eat without sass.
Whilst he calls me the best of good fellows,
Most egregiously he'll be an ass.
He'll pull the wool out of his head
When about his wife all's understood—
For I'll swear black is white[46]—'fore they married,
She jilted the whole neighborhood.

Exeunt, R. H.

❧

Scene 5. Stage ¾ dark. Enter Otello, Cassio, *and* attendants, R. H.
    Otello
You, Massa Michael, who am always right,
While I go roost, you keep the watch tonight.
And don't you wake me morrow morning soon—
I shan't get up much 'fore the arternoon.

Exit C. D. *with attendants*

Iago *enters* L. H. *as* Otello *exits*

    Cassio
By my soul, Iago, I must to my post.
    Iago
Why, how you talk, 'tisn't ten, at most.
Otello's early: Well, and so he oughter,
For Desdemona. She's a regular snorter.

Cassio

She's a charming eye—

Iago

                        Oh, Cassio, fie—

And yet, you're right: Scissors, what an eye!

Cassio

Faith, she's right modest though—

Iago

                            I think no less.

Let's go and liquor and drink their happiness!

Cassio

Sir, not to night—I've already had a toddy.

Another one would soon capsize the body.

Iago

Pooh, nonsense, man—we'll find here at the lunch

Plenty who'll join us in a whiskey punch.

Cassio

Well, just one glass—Devil the more I'll take.

                            Enter Montano *and* Ludovico[47]

Cassio

Here's health to Desdemona and Otello—

Although he's black, he's a devilish good fellow.

Come, Iago, as I can't stop here long,

Suppose you tip us just a little song.

Iago

With all my heart

                Air—"Corn Cobs"[48]

          Come fill the Can

          And I'm the man

          Will challenge anybody

          To sing all night

          Till broad daylight

And drink fine apple toddy.

Then let the can go clink, clink, clink!

We'll never think of shrinking.

While there's a drop we'll never stop,

But go ahead on drinking.

    Cassio

A capital song! [*sings*]

A very good song and very well sung,

Jolly companions, every one.

I say, Iago, where did you learn that strain?

    Iago

In Massachusetts, next to the State of Maine.[49]

They're the chaps for drinking, what a swallow,

They beat New York and Philadelphy Boys all hollow.

    Cassio

Faith, it's right good stuff—it makes me frisky.

No doubt it's "Cuter Cousin" to good old whiskey.

    Iago

    Air—"Gabby Glum"[50]

To cheer the spirits up,

There's nothing like a good whiskey.

Jist you take a sip,

It makes you feel so frisky.

It gladdens up the heart

Jist to whet the throttle;

And never more will part—

Your mouth and this sweet bottle.

    Both join in Chorus

    Cassio

That's a more exquisite song, Sir, than the first.

'Tis strange how drinking does improve one's thirst.

Iago, I'll thank you for another swig.

If we'd the lasses here, wouldn't we have a jig?

Well, Saint Patrick help us! We must drink, you see.

The Captain, he must drink as well as we.

There are some folks, to be sure, can't drink;

And there are some that can—I'm one, I think.

Iago

Guess I am, too. [*about to drink*]

Cassio

                  Not before me, Sir, if you please.

I'm senior officer—in my own right I seize.

                                    Enter Roderigo, R. H.

Roderigo

He's getting drunk.

Cassio

Drunk! That word again dare speak,

I'll knock you in the middle of next week.

Drunk? And it's me that's drunk, you said?

Isn't this your fist and isn't that my head?

                          Takes off coat and prepares for a fight

Roderigo

He smells of whiskey worse than any skunk.

Why, what a shame to get so horrid drunk.

Cassio

Ah, ha! That's twice I'm drunk! You just wait awhile

And maybe I won't polish you off in style.

Iago

Stick to him only for a round or so,

And I'll put out and let Otello know. [*exit* c.d.]

[*Music.* Roderigo *and* Cassio *fight. Enter* Iago *and knocks* Roderigo *down from behind. Enter four* supers *with torches.* Otello *enters and*

beats the whole party. Roderigo's *face is covered with blood.* Cassio *has
a black eye:* Otello *has a stuffed stick*]

Otello

[*Recitative*] Hold for your lives. Why, how is this? Am we turned
   Turks to scratch and fight and to ourselves do dat which am for-
   bid de common loafer? He dat strikes anoder blow I'll butt him
   all to pieces. Dat noisy bell, stop him[51] clatter.

Air—"French"

Otello

Iago, who began dis spice?
Dis instant tell me who's to blame—
And 'dough de chap was twin'd wid me
Dat moment he lose all de claim.

Second Verse

Montano, is you drunk or mad?
Your conduct used to be so civil,
But now you so damn bad—
You're worser den de bery Devil.

Third Verse

How comes it, Michael, you mistake
To get so drunk and leff your passion loose?
I had a good notion for to take
And put you in de calaboose.

Montano

Oh! What a blow in the ribs—that was a poser.

Roderigo

Pshaw! What's a blow in the ribs? Look at my nose, sir!

[*exit* L. H.]

Otello

Come speak, Iago, none of dis here nonsense.
Tell me de truth, at once, and ease your conscience.

Air—"My Long Tail Blue"[52]

Iago

I had rather my tongue was cut slick out

Than speak ought to offend this youth.

But if you insist to know what 'tis about,

Why, I guess then I'll best tell the truth.

[*chorus*] I guess then I'd best tell the truth. [*repeat four times*]

Second Verse

Thus it is: we were taking a glass of Stone Fence[53]

Good Montano, myself, and a friend.

And, when once in the liquor we 'gan to commence,

Why, we thought we'll just drink to the end.

[*chorus*] I guess then I'd best tell the truth. [*repeat four times*]

Third Verse

Now Cassio, you see, had swallowed all down.

And by this time had got rather blue.

When a fellow comes crying, "There's a fire downtown—

Turn out, turn out, twenty two."[54]

[*chorus*] I guess then I'd best tell the truth. [*repeat four times*]

Fourth Verse

In returning, I saw that young gentleman there

Give Cassio a blow in the eye.

I did all in my power to stop the affair,

But their fury my aid did defy.

[*chorus*] I guess then I'd best tell the truth. [*repeat four times*]

Fifth Verse

Then to it they went. But, my friend do forgive.

For you know, Sir, that men are but men.

And, if you'll excuse him, my word I will give

That he never will do so again.

[*chorus*] I guess then I'd best tell the truth. [*repeat four times*]

Otello

Cassio [*crosses to him*] to you, Iago bery partial.

So I discharge you widout de court martial.

Iago

Oh, good Otello, put on him a fine.

Otello

Cassio neber more be ossifer ob mine.

                              exit Otello and attendants

Iago

Come, come, friend Cassio, where's the use—tarnation.

Cassio

My reputation lost, my reputation.

I'm bothered, Sir. I'm bothered, quite, with thinking

I've lost my reputation, Sir, with drinking.

I, who in punch ne'er flinched to any body,

Drunk and bewildered with an apple toddy.

Was ever man in such a situation?

Oh, blood an' 'ouns, I've lost my reputation. [*crosses* R. H.]

Iago

Why, how you talk! Guess we can mend your reputation—

Your stomach was a leetle out of calculation.

Cassio

Oh, that the devil thus should dwell in toddy,

To steal men's brains and then capsize the body.

What shall I do to ease my mind of pain?

Iago

Suppose you ask him for your place again?

I have it! Go and make some pretty speeches

To Mrs. O. You know she wears the breeches.

Come the soft sodder.[55] And if you find she freezes,

Don't be afraid, give her a few sly squeezes

Until her bosom thaws. Then she will plead;
And, if she does, the place is yours, indeed.

Cassio [crosses, L. H.]

Tis a glorious scheme. I'll do it! Thank ye.
A plan that's really worthy of a Yankee.
By the powers, it is the way. You're right.
I thank you much, my friend, and so good night.

Shakes hands and exits L. H.

As Cassio *exits*, Roderigo *enter*, R. H.

Iago

How do ye do?

Roderigo

About so so, how get you on?

Iago

A little longer and the thing is done.
Listen!

Air—"Oats, Beans and Barley oh"

Iago

I guess at last I've found a plan
Where in you'll say that I'm the man
Can do just what no other can
In female speculation.
Otello shall his wife divorce,
Kase Cassio's held with her discourse,
And then, my boy, she's your's, of course,
Beyond all calculation.

Second Verse

While Cassio kneels with all his grace
To Desdemona for his place,
Otello shall meet him face to face
And the fat will be in the fire.

OTELLO 145

Then they'll be in a pretty fix—
With their broken hearts, with their thumping sticks.
As long as there'll be plenty of kicks,
It's all that we desire.

Exeunt L. H.

⤐⤏

Scene 6. Room in castle. Sofa R. H.

Enter Desdemona, Emilia *and* Cassio R. H.

Desdemona

I'll ask him when he's had a glass or two.
There's no one, I'd do more for, Sir, than you.

Emilia

That's a good soul. She'll bring the thing about.
Oh, Sir, my poor dear husband's much put out.

Desdemona

You're a good chap. The Moor'll be home to sup.
I'll tease him, 'til he says he'll make it up.

Cassio

But stress my place. If we're not sure today,
The chances are he'll give my place away.

Desdemona

Don't fret yourself. Here, before her face,
I promise you that you shall have your place.
I'll tease him so, he ne'er shall hear the last, Sir,
So don't you stew.

Emilia

Madam, here comes my master.

Cassio

Oh, then I'm off . . . [*crosses* R.]

Desdemona

Don't be a fool, pray stop.

Cassio

I can't—I tremble so that I shall drop.

exits R. H.

Enter Otello *and* Iago L. H.

Otello reading newspaper

Iago

He here! I don't half like that.

Otello

What's dat you say—

Iago

Nothing, I spoke to the cat.

Otello

Was not dat Cassio, parted from my wife?

Iago

I do not think 'twas him, upon my life.

What reason, Sir, should he, or any one,

Seeing you, cut stick, clear out and run?

Otello

I do belibe 'twas him, for see ...

Iago

Perhaps your wife has axed him home to tea?

Otello

Missus Otello, who is dat to whom you speak?

And why—when I come in—away he sneak?

Desdomona

The fact is, Ducky, bless your snowball face,[56]

'Twas Cassio pleading to get back his place.

If you refuse me—then the news that next is

Cassio's off and making tracks for Texas.
Shall I run after him and say you will?
  Otello
No, not tonight. I feel so rader queerish ill.
  Desdemona
Well, then tomorrow morning, or at noon,
Or else tomorrow night, or sometime soon.
Say Wednesday morning then—or noon—or night.
I'll take compassion on the luckless night.
Well, Thursday? Friday? Saturday or Sunday?
At most you'll not defer it after Monday.
Why how is this, Otello? Speak Sir, pray.
  Otello
Why, leff him come and all will be O.K.

                                    Exeunt Desdemona *and* Emilia R. H.
  Otello
De way I lub her really is a sin
And, when I doesn't, chaos comed again[57] [*crosses* L.]
  Iago
General, did Cassio know you really lov'd her so?
  Otello
Yes, be sure he did, what for you wish to know?
  Iago
Indeed. [*winks*]
  Otello
Indeed! What for you wink your eye?
And cry, indeed, and look so bery shy—
Am he not honest?
  Iago
Honest, my lord? [*looking up*]

Otello

Yes, honest.

Iago

  As well as this world kin afford.

Otello

What do you tink?

Iago

                    Think, my dear Otello?

Why, then, I think, Cassio an honest fellow.

Otello

I tink so too. But dat's no news to tell.

You don't tink so, I know bery well.

You tink him tief!

Iago

                    I think him something worse.

Otello

Aye! You tink he pick your pocket or your purse.

Iago

Who steals my purse steals trash.[58] Look here a minute:

There once was something; now there's nothing in it.

Twas his, 'tis mine, and been in all disasters.

But never hold again, I fear shinplasters:[59]

Cassio, I guess, would aim at higher game;

He'd sign a check in any man's good name

To take my all. Oh, how my heart doth bleed!

I would make him rich but leave me poor indeed.

Otello

Iago, you mean someting 'pon my life.

I tink, you tink Cassio lub my wife.

No, Massa Iago, I prove before I doubt;

And when I prove, why den I sarbe her out.

If she lubs Cassio and not me, I find,
I'll whistle her off and leff her down the wind.[60] [*crosses* L.]
    Iago
You're right. Wear your eyes open; look to your wife.
I wouldn't have you jealous for my life,
But she's a critter, here in Venice bred;[61]
Her father she deceived in marrying you—'nuf sed.
    Otello
Why, so she did.
    Iago
               —You seem a little dashed or so.
    Otello
[*crosses* R. H.] No, I assure you, not a jot. No, no.
    Iago
I now must leave you, Gineral, and what's going on
You'll hear from me, you may depend upon.
                [*Exits* L., *crosses* L.]
    Otello
Why did I marry? More could Iago chat,
If he'd but let de bag out of de cat.
         [*plays with tassel*]
           Re-enter Iago L. *to* R.
    Iago
Gineral, I've just stepped back to beg that you'll incline
To scan this thing no further. Leave it all to time.
Don't let what I have said put you in a flurry;
And don't fill Cassio's place up in a hurry.
If much your wife in Cassio's interest takes
It's my opinion, then, she's no "great shakes."
    Otello
I'll watch her close.

Iago

Once more, adieu. [*going*]

Otello

Iago, I am much obliged to you. [*exit* Iago L. H.]

Enter Desdemona *with towel,* R. H.

Desdemona

Come, come, Otello. Recollect, I pray.

You asked some folks to take pot luck today;

They're all arrived and only wait for you.

Come and receive you guests, Otello do.

Otello

I'm not quite well. My head hab got a pain.

Desdemona

Why that's with watching; 'twill be well again.

Here, let me bind this towel round it tight

And you shall take some Brandreth's Pills tonight.

Otello

De towel am too little [*puts it away*] dat neber mine,

Let it alone. Come, I'll go in to dine.

Exeunt

Emilia *enters as they exit*

Emilia

I'm glad I've found this towel on the floor.

This was her first remembrance from the Moor.

My husband wants it—I can't tell why or wherefore;

This is not stealing. What did he throw it there for?

Enter Iago, L. H.

Iago

What on earth are you hovering here about?

Emilia

What's that to you? You may go find out.

Iago

You're a nice one.

Emilia

                              Oh am I, very well,

Then what I've got for you I shall not tell.

Iago

For me? What can you have for me?

Emilia

If you speak prettily you shall see.

Iago

Why, how you talk.

Emilia

                              Well, a towel then.

Iago

What towel?

Emilia

                    Desdemona's—don't you ken?

Iago

Oh Scissors![62] The one Otello gave her, let me see.

That's a good critter [*snatches it*] give it to me.

Now travel!

Emilia

        Oh, let me put it in its place:

She's got no other towel to wipe her face.

Iago

Clear out!

                    Exit Emilia, R. H.

Iago

I'll just put this towel in Mr. Cassio's room,

And, when discovered, she'll be a gone coon.

Enter Otello, *his wool all on end.*[63] Seizes Iago and butts him.

Otello

False, false to me, villain, be sure you prove what you hab said,

Or else, Iago, much better you be dead.

Iago

If this fact ain't enough, then call me dunce.

Did you not give your wife a towel once?

Otello

Yes, I did. What you hab me understand?

Iago

This morning, with it, Cassio wiped his hand.

Otello

Enough! I'll tear her all to pieces, Sar, like dis,

Dow she'd as many lives as de tom cat.

Don't let dis ar matter go no furder:

Us two, 'dem two, will murder.

You kill Cassio, you hab him place;

And Desdemona, I'll spoil her face.

Air—"Dandy Jim"[64]

A Gypsy woman, whose name was Cowell

To my poor moder gib'd dat towel.[65]

And, if she lose or gib it away,

Wid my father, she would fight all day.

chorus De Gypsy woman tell me so,

I was born to be a General, oh.

I looked in the glass and find it so,

Jist what de Gypsy told me, oh.

Second Verse

De towel was made of raccoon hide

And in de bakehouse often dried,

'Twas washed and bleached wid coconut milk,

And sewed and hemmed with hot cornsilk.

chorus

Third Verse

I did not care if all de camp,
   De Gineral, province, and rank,
   De fifer and de drummer, oh,
   Hab kissed her—so I did not know.

chorus

Fourth Verse

To lub a wife dat don't lub me,
I'd rather be a toad, you see;
And den de face to lib upon
De wassous ob a demijohn.

chorus

"Air." Otello kneels

Farewell to de banjo and de cymbals,
De drum, fife, and trumpet loud swell;
Farewell to de jaw bone and jingles,
De fiddle and jew's harp, farewell.
Farewell to de mind dat was quiet
And de big wars whar laurels am won.
Farewell joy, pride, pomp and come riot:
Otello's occupation am gone.

"Air"

Come now Iago, go wid me
And put some pisen in shoushong tea
And gib to Desdemony
And make her drink it up.
And for her Irish crony
He too shall hab a sup.

Iago

If you will pisen her, we're sure to swing.

I'll just propose another thing:

We'll say the cat had bit her.

 She went mad and broke our heads;

 And so we took the critter

 And we smother'd her 'tween two beds.

Otello

Iago, I'm oblige to you

Dat's de bery ting I'll do.

We'll smoder her like fury,

And I shall git divorce,

And den de judge and jury

We will not pay, in course.

Exeunt L. H.

➤❤

Scene 7. Bed in C.: Desdemona asleep. Cradle and child[66] *in it,* L. H. *Soft Music.*[67] *Enter* Otello *with candle,* L.

   Otello

It am de cause,   *caw—caw—caw*[68]

It am de cause.   *caw—caw—caw*

Let me not tell you ob it, oh you lubly stars,

It am de cause.   *caw—caw—caw*

Yes, she must die, dat is plain,

Else more niggers she'll betray again.

Put out dy light, why den dow ain't candle, still,

And I can light dee up, jist at my will.

Put out dy light, sweet Desdemony.

Why den, indeed, it all day wid dee, Honey.

But wives, you see, should neber do amiss.

And now me gib de last, de last fond kiss.

Approaches to kiss, when she kicks him over[69]

> Desdemona

Who's there? Oh, dear me, is it you, Otello?

> Otello

You're right. It am indeed dat much-abused poor fellow.

Tell me, Desdemona, and tell me right,

Hab you, Honey, said your prayers to night?

And since dat kick jist now from you I tuck it,

You now, my lub, hab got to kick de bucket.

> Desdemona

Talk you of killing? Oh, for mercy's sake!

> Otello

It are a fact—and no mistake.[70]

> Desdemona

Otello, you are jealous—that's the truth—

Of Michael Cassio, the poor dear youth.

> Otello

Dear youth! Dear debil! Why you call him dear,

Here, to my face, my eye, my ear?

Dat towel you gib to Cassio—well I know it.

> Desdemona

Upon my life and soul, I didn't do it.

Now ain't you quizzing?

> Otello

                                      True, as here I sit.

Why, damn you, I seed de towel, seed Cassio using it.[71]

> Desdemona

Some towel like it, p'raps. How should you know?

Otello

Kase, in de corner, dars de 'nitial O.

Desdemona

Send for Michael Cassio.

Otello

Send for Michael Debil O—He can't come at all,

Kase he hab put him spoon into de wall.[72]

Desdemona

Dead, ah, I can't help crying for the lad.

Otello

What, cry before my face? [*rises*] Dat's too damn bad.

[*seizes the bed: child cries*] Hush you damn jaw.

Desdemona

Kill me tomorrow: let me live to night.

If you come near me, I'll scratch and bite. [*knock* L. H.]

Emilia [*outside*]

Oh, my good lord, I'd speak a word with you:

There's been foul murder done! What shall we do?

Otello

Here's some one coming, dar's no use of kicking.

You must be smuddered 'tween dese ar bed ticking.

Desdemona

Give me but half an hour.

Otello

—not as you knows on.

Desdemona

A minute while I pray.

Otello

Take care den, dis goes on.

Smothers her with bed. Enter all the characters except Roderigo.

Music—"Dan Tucker"[73]
Emilia
Oh, good, my lord, in town this night,
There has been such a desperate fight:
Michael Cassio with a blow
Has laid poor Roderigo low.

Chorus Bring them along before Otello,
Cassio, Rod and the other fellow.
Bring them along before Otello,
Cassio, Rod and the other fellow.

Otello
Roderigo dead and Cassio libing,
To desperation I am driben,
For what I've done, dar's no forgiben.
Eh, eh, eh! Good bye, wife.

Chorus

Chorus
Oh you hateful, ugly fellow:
After killing Mrs. Otello,
You may cry and moan and bellow,
With your "Eh, eh, eh! Good bye, wife."

Chorus

Otello   Alma Opera[74]
One word before you go:
I hab you for to know
I done de state some sarbice,
And de foe hab laid her low.
And, when you dis relate,
Noten extenuate,
But merely say, Good lack,

If his wife hab but been black,
Instead of white, all had been right
And she wouldn't hab got de sack.
 So, now, if it please your will,
 I'll go to de Treaden Mill. [*Gong*]
  Desdemona comes to life and pops up
   Chorus—"Fifth July"[75]
Oh, look here; Oh, look there!
Desdemona's come to life:
See her rise and ope her eyes.
Otello's once more got his wife.
Then dance and sing
'Till the whole house ring,
And never more his wife he'll smother.
And, if all right tomorrow night,
We'll have this wedding over.
      Repeat
    Dance by all the Characters
     Curtain[76]

Notes

Selected Bibliography

Notes

Songs

1. "The Original Jim Crow" as published by E. Riley in New York at 29 Chatham Street, probably 1832.

2. There are many Tuckahoe place names. Perhaps the most famous, and patent for many others, is the plantation where Thomas Jefferson grew up because his father managed the estate. It is still preserved, on the banks of the Tuckahoe Creek, a tributary of the James River ten miles west of Richmond, Virginia. See Jessie Thompson Krusen, "Tuckahoe Plantation," in *Winterthur Portfolio 11*, edited by Ian M. G. Quimby (Charlottesville: University Press of Virginia, Published for The Henry Francis du Pont Winterthur Museum, 1976), 103–122.

3. Nicolo Paganini (1788–1840), Italian violin virtuoso, was the proverbial model of excellence.

4. Major General Edward Pakenham commanded the British forces invading New Orleans in the culminating battle of the War of 1812. General Andrew Jackson massacred Pakenham and more than 2,000 of his troops on 8 January 1814. Until the Civil War, most American theatres mounted special celebratory events on the anniversary of the Battle of New Orleans.

5. Viper.

6. Unleavened cornmeal batter, baked on a hoe before a fire.

7. In other words, if white workers worked honest days, like slaves, then Constable Hays, the legendary historical figure in New York City, would have no one to arrest.

8. Daniel Lambert (1770–1809), born in Leicester, exhibited himself in London and elsewhere in England during the last three years of his life when he weighed over 700 lbs. His weight at his death was 739 lbs. For an image, see Richard D. Altick, *The Shows of London* (Cambridge, Mass.: The Belknap Press of Harvard University Press, 1978), 254.

9. I have transcribed this complex song from a double broadside (now at The Library Company of Philadelphia). It prints "Jim Crow, Still Alive!!!" on one side and "Dinah Crow" facing and perhaps answering it on the other, both "Sold by B. Brammel, No. 572, North Second street; and by Johnson Scarlett, 8, Market street Philadelphia." This statement of responsibility is printed twice, once beneath each song. Dinah Crow was fast becoming a specialty of Dan Gardner, who was appearing in Philadelpia neighborhoods (the Northern Liberties) in J. B. Green's Menagerie and Circus in the fall of 1835, singing "The Extravaganza of Dinah Crow" (see playbill at the Historical Society of Pennsylvania). Dan Gardner went on to specialize in "wench" parts in New York and Philadelphia.

This broadside illustrates the fundamental vexation on which lumpen popular culture has often thrived. It presents two styles of storytelling and versemaking. Rice's Jim Crow verses generally present an action contained and completely told in one verse. When his topics extend to successive verses, each one presents a discrete action. Gardner's Dinah Crow verses narrate part of a story that will go on for several stanzas before the topic alters, and separate actions spread across verses. The broadside presents an argument between two street characters, much as if—in our time—they were enacting the dozens.

Only "Jim Crow, Still Alive!!!" is printed here. For Dinah's answer to Jim Crow see *Jump Jim Crow: Lost Plays, Lyrics, and Street Prose of the First Atlantic Popular Culture* (Cambridge, Mass.: Harvard University Press, 2003), pp. 116–127.

10. Edwin Williams, ed., *New-York as It Is in 1833; and Citizens Advertising Directory* (New York: J. Disturnell, 1833), 143.

11. The New York City policeman whose coralling of wayward youths was legendary.

12. New York's city government was known as the "Corporation."

13. Champagne.

14. Reverend Ephraim K. Avery. This Methodist minister in Bristol, Rhode Island was accused of murdering Sarah M. Cornell, a factory worker, near Fall River, Massachusetts, 22 December 1832. He was tried in 6 May 1833 and news of his acquittal hit the newspapers one month later, 5 June 1833 (as in the *American Sentinel*, col. 1, p. 2). See Thomas M. McDade, comp., *The Annals of Murder: A Bibliography of Books and Pamphlets on American Murders from Colonial Times to 1900* (Norman, Okla.: University of Oklahoma Press, 1961), 13–18.

15. Catharine Market, where T. D. Rice was born and raised in New York City's Seventh Ward, was built on a swamp; tuberculosis and yellow fever raged through the Ward many summers.

16. Address of the publisher: B. Brammell, Philadelphia.

17. See note 8.

18. Patch was an early daredevil and falls jumper. He jumped the Passaic Falls on 30 September 1827, then jumped Niagara Falls several times, saying "Some things can be done as well as others," which became a cant phrase. He died in a jump on Friday the 13th of November, 1829 at the 99-foot Upper Falls at Rochester, New York. Friends and small crowds had seen him jump these falls more than once successfully, but this time he was inebriated from preliminary festivity; he dislocated both shoulders on impact and could not swim to safety; he was found dead in the ice the next spring.

19. Drinking cup.

20. "Stone Fence" was one of the earliest American mixed drinks: brandy and cider.

21. *The Negro Forget-Me-Not Songster; the Only Work Published, Containing All the Negro Songs That Have Ever Appeared* (Philadelphia: Turner & Fisher, 1844), 247–249; said there to be "Sung by the celebrated Tom Rice."

22. See note 20.

23. This reference dates this verse, if not the song, to 1836, the year Van Buren was elected and Rice went to London.

24. Leonard Deming was a prolific publisher of Jim Crow lyrics in Boston. The American Antiquarian Society, in particular, holds several different sheets of Jim Crow lyrics Deming printed as broadsides. This one dates to 1837–1840, when Deming was at 61 Hanover Street, Boston.

25. Long Island Juba.

26. Although the lyrics did not proliferate as wildly as they did in "Jim Crow," many versions of "Clare de Kitchen" entered print. This early example, published in Baltimore by John Cole, was transcribed from a copy in the DeVincent Collection at the Smithsonian.

27. Soldiers' clothes.

28. One of the most persistent stereotypes of wench characters in blackface is their grotesque flatfootedness, here going beyond flat to a convex stump.

29. Cucumber.

30. There were many printings of "Gumbo Chaff." This one by George Willig, Jr. in Baltimore is early. The variants I have seen retain the stanzas in order as here, although there are frequent changes in spelling, pronoun number (we for I), small details, and lines.

31. This version is "Sold by L. Deming . . . Boston" and must date between 1832–1837.

32. There were many versions of this popular minstrel song. This one is attributed to Dan Emmett's group, The Virginia Minstrels, and was published by F. D. Benteen, Baltimore, 1846.

33. "A celebrated Comic Extravaganza as Sung at the Theatres," published by J. A. L. Hewitt & Co., 239 Broadway, New York.

Plays

Virginia Mummy

1. Rice's prompt script for *Virginia Mummy* exists in a scribe's hand as British Library Add MSS 42940, ff. 822–867. The script dates the first performance as 22 April 1835 in Mobile, Alabama, and the Mobile *Commercial Register* confirms that Noah Ludlow's benefit took place that night: the play was "Written especially for the occasion, by Mr. Rice." The MS lists this original cast:

Ginger Blue	Mr. Rice
Galen	Mr. Marks
Rifle	Mr. Ruddell
[Ch]arles	Mr. Thompson
[O']Leary	Mr. Johnson
Paitent (sic)	Mr. Barclay
Schoolmaster	Mr. La Rue

Servant	Mr. Bacon
Porter	Mr. Hartman
Lucy	Minnick
Susan	Graham

Rice also played *Virginia Mummy* at least in Philadelphia, Boston, and New Orleans before he took it to England, where he opened it at the Royal Surrey on 1 August 1836. Plays for theatres south of the Thames, such as the Surrey, did not have to pass the censor. Thus it was not until Rice wanted to play *Virginia Mummy* at Covent Garden, north of the river, that he submitted it to the Lord Chamberlain. Rice submitted the play to the censor and performed it at Covent Garden on the same day, 13 March 1837; the Lord Chamberlain did not approve it until after the production, on the 15th. *Virginia Mummy* became a staple of the blackface Christy Minstrels as well as the expatriate black actor Ira Aldridge.

    Much later, Charles White published two different adaptations of the play, neither dated. White's Happy Hours text is closer to the MS than is the Dick & Fitzgerald text. The latter begins with a different speech by Rifle, omits the first two scene changes, and sets all the early business in front of the hotel. The prompt script MS at the British Library is the best text of the play: it is full of Rice's business, his attitudes, his jokes. Unfortunately, a tear has obliterated its very ending. Thus I have completed the play by following the last few lines of the Happy Hours text. In the Historical Society of Pennsylvania, there is also a manuscript for the version of the play that the Christy Minstrels performed; its events are much the same, with some of the names and business changed. I have used this Christy *Mummy* to help determine the performed core of the play.

    2. Patent leather; but perhaps this is a description of style, too, for "patent" also meant "open." This is the first play on "patent," meaning "licensed," in a script that regularly pokes fun at legitimacy.

    3. A nineteenth-century plastic, caoutchouc was derived from the *Hevea brasiliensis* tree of South America and vulcanized with sulfur. An early example of a consumer technology become all the rage, it indicated Rifle's metropolitan manners.

    4. Note the pun on exit/ax't.

    5. Love letter.

    6. In the British Library manuscript, a pencil has slashed the speech from this dash to its end.

7. See *Bone Squash Diavolo,* where Junietta tells Bone "de warm wedder hab so opened de paws of my system dat de perspiration flows just as copiously as de lasses from de hogshead" (1.2).

8. The Roman physician Galen (A.D. 130–200) made important contributions in several medical fields. His was an early voice in scientific racism, stating that "blacks inherited defective brains" and cataloguing stereotypes that became the classic delineators of black difference. See S. C. Drake, *Black Folk Here and There: An Essay in History and Anthropology,* vol. 2 (Los Angeles: Center for Afro-American Studies, University of California, 1987), p. 56; David Brion Davis, *Slavery and Human Progress* (New York: Oxford University Press, 1984), p. 42; and W. Michael Byrd and Linda A. Clayton, *An American Health Dilemma, Volume One, A Medical History of African Americans and the Problem of Race: Beginnings to 1900* (New York: Routledge, 2000), pp. 70–73. Rice and Ginger Blue targeted Dr. Galen for their sharpest ridicule.

9. Monkey (Jack) from Naples—an ethnic slur.

10. The settlement at Stonington was claimed both by Massachusetts and Connecticut in the mid-seventeenth century; it suffered naval attacks by the British during the Revolutionary War (1775) and again in 1814, during the War of 1812. Galen's chronology is as confused as his royal history. The various editions of the play substitute other battles.

11. Charles White gives, for Rice's "perplexing": *perfect stupid.*

12. Good will, aid.

13. Rice is playing on the often-repeated scene of slaves believing books talk to their readers. Ginger Blue hides within an image of blacks that Ginger knows Rifle will find credible.

14. The devil.

15. This conceit of mixing paint ingredients to represent race remains in play in the performance of American race at least up through Ralph Ellison's *Invisible Man* (1952) and its scene at the Liberty Paint factory (ch. 10). The mixture had more colors in the early nineteenth century than in the middle of the twentieth.

16. In the British Library manuscript, the stage manager has inked in here "Song Mr. Rice before change" and someone else has blocked in "Jim Crow" in pencil. Both of Charles White's adaptations indicate a "song" before the scene changes. But it is clear the song was not scripted in the original production; Ginger's remark, and the song he sang, register the entrepreneurial expectations that built up around Rice's performances, as around the representation of blackness at every level.

17. Holding out the boa.

18. Pointing to Charles's painting.

19. In 1773, J. Hawkesworth compiled the journals of James Cook's three principal journeys into *An Account of a Voyage Round the World, 1768–1771.*

20. In what may be Rice's hand, the MS has "ham" crossed out and replaced with "hog." "Hoggler" or "hogler" was an old word for a field worker of the lowest class; blacks were often said to be "smoked."

21. As in London and other cities, Philadelphia police had boxes at corners to protect them from the weather. They were sites of legendary pranks for streetwise youths, who would try to knock the cubicles over, especially with a policeman in them, preferably door-side down.

22. The joke in Rice's blackface theatre was that the black effect was produced by shoe polish. This is one of many references to the artificiality of the representation in Rice's performances that co-exist with simultaneous insistence on his authentic mimesis.

23. This last phrase in the stage directions is inserted in Rice's hand and double-underlined.

24. From the end of this line, for almost three and a half MS pages, until O'Leary announces the arrival of Patent and the new mummy, a pencil line has crossed out the text. The edition of the play that Charles White published in the 1880s omitted this passage, as crossed out. But much of the business in the deleted passage was clearly set up earlier, and several of the remarks that follow the omitted passage make no sense without it, so I am re-inserting it again—on the grounds that the original play, performed in Mobile, included this material.

25. Galen is expressing the same prejudice toward the Irish as was conventionally expressed toward blacks, and which Ginger Blue has just fulfilled.

26. *Laid in the mighty hetacombs:* in his excitement, Galen is compounding "catacomb" (underground tomb) with "hetaera" (a concubine).

27. Dead or sold south.

28. Amalgamation was the contemporary term for interracial mixing.

29. This is the end of the excised passage.

30. Woodchuck.

31. A hollow tree in which bees make their hives; often it was a black gum tree.

32. Dubious.

33. Someone has penciled over "before de She nigga," with "before Queen Shebera"; and White gives "before de Queen Sherbera."

Bone Squash

1. This composite text combines the manuscript of the 1839 one-act version Rice performed in London, *Bone Squash: A Burletta* (British Library Add MSS 42953, ff. 312–319), with Charles White's thrice-published editions, which he called *Bone Squash: A Comic Opera* (New York: Fredric A. Brady, n.d.; New York: Happy Hours Company, n.d.; New York: Samuel French, n.d.). In choosing among these variants, three factors determined my solutions. First, I wanted to give as full a text as possible. Thus, if there was no reason to doubt that Rice performed a scene in the adaptation by White, I included it. Second, when the short version conflicted with the longer printed texts, I preferred the one-act version because that was certainly the bare spine of the play, beyond which Rice would not cut; after all, the prompt script was in his own hand. And finally, I could check these four texts against long scene descriptions from early playbills in the United States and in London, and I had a letter from Rice to Francis Wemyss (11 September 1835, at the Harvard Theatre Collection) explaining the play's internal difficulties that prohibited its timely opening in Philadelphia. These early descriptions and their attendant cast lists indicate slippages, as well as continuity, among Rice's productions and White's.

2. "Duck legs" referred to a known posture in contemporary Philadelphia slang: "With a thick piece of cord reaching from one calf to another, [one character's duck legs] would have described the letter A; as they rubbed together at the knees, and were separated by the space of a foot between the boots" (George Lippard, *The Quaker City, or, The Monks of Monk Hall,* edited by David S. Reynolds, reprint, 1845 [Amherst: University of Massachusetts Press, 1995], p. 427).

3. In his Adelphi script, Rice cut the song to this single verse, made the pronouns plural, and gave it as the initial chorus, sung as the curtain rose.

4. The Park Theatre was New York's society theatre in the 1830s, at which no bootblack, sweep, or whitewasher—and few members of Rice's public—would have felt welcome.

5. Nicolo Paganini (1788–1840), the Italian violin virtuoso, was the gold standard for genius in Atlantic popular culture during these decades.

6. Rice early billed this song as "I Am the Paganini" (Surrey playbill, 15 July 1836, British Library Playbills, vol. 313). By 19 June 1840, he was listing it on playbills as "I Am de Child ob Genus" (Bowery Folder, Harvard Theatre Collection). Another version of this frequent blackface song appears at the

end of E. P. Christy, *Christy's Plantation Melodies (Book No. 3)* (Philadelphia: Fisher & Brother, 1853) as "Jim Brown's Address to His Sogers."

7. Charles White's texts give "log" here, but Rice's MS clearly reads "lag." The lag is the calm interval between tidal rushes, when optimal crossings occurred. Here, Bone is doubtless referring to the ferry between Catherine Market and Brooklyn. Rice grew up at Catherine Market, later lived in Brooklyn, and was buried in its Greenwood Cemetery.

8. *Ely's Hawk and Buzzard, or, New-York, Saturday Courier and Enquirer By Johannes Vanderdecken* began in 1832. Their slogan: "Our Gossip Birds Shall Keep a Bright Look Out And Show The World What Folly Is About." Their lead editorial on the occasion of their return to publication on 1 September 1832:

> It is well known by all unprejudiced persons, that the paper had a tendency to keep a certain class of beings under subjection through fear of having their deeds exposed by our *vigilant* BIRDS. The *spreeing blades* whose midnight revels so oft have disturbed the quiet slumbers of our peaceful citizens, were selected out as food for our *Buzzard*. We were ever on the watch—faithful and fearless—with a full determination to ferret out the secret movements of our city authorities, that we might lay their proceedings before our readers on each Saturday . . . It shall be our duty to seek out every sink of infamy; that on each Saturday we may give the character of the inmates of these modern *hells* to our readers.
>
> We shall pay particular attention to the streets, see that all nuisances are removed, as we intend to make a St[reet]. Inspector of the Buzzard, who will remove every infected carcass from the city. . . . The hawk will explore every part of Gotham, seeking out intelligence; and woe be to the *wretch* who falls within the grasp of his *talons!*

One cannot read too far in the *Hawk and Buzzard* (the best run is at the American Antiquarian Society) without realizing that it is a much more politically chocked forerunner to *Mad Magazine*. The *Hawk and Buzzard* is written in code, making itself up as it goes. It revolves around the lower East Side between Coenties Slip and Pearl Street (pretty much the circle Bone describes in his first speech). It is no accident that the paper is full of references to Jim Crow, for its readership is the literate portion of Rice's public. Like the Jim Crow plays, the *Hawk and Buzzard* maps the Catherine Market mentality.

9. The New York *Mirror*, a middlebrow literary magazine, had as its original subtitle, "Ladies Literary Gazette"; Rice had feuded with the *Mirror* since they published an attack on *Oh! Hush!* on 5 October 1833; for more on this conflict, see the Introduction in *Jump Jim Crow*, under the heading "Gumbo Cuff and the New York Desdemonas."

10. "Rhino" was street slang for money.

11. The protocols of "treating" were obligatory and paramount in working class culture; when Rice shortened this duet for his one-act version, he began with this verse, followed only by the Devil's last four lines at the end of the song.

12. Pest imagery clusters around the Jim Crow characters; they fight the war of the flea.

13. See Figure 2.

14. An equivalent to "Say, calf rope" or, "Say, Uncle"—except that it refers to the primary fight between brothers, Cain and Abel.

15. Joseph L. Hays was a legendary police officer in New York City, and the youth culture's bugaboo. His resignation from his position of police marshall in early 1833 was noticed in newspapers at least as distant as Philadelphia (*Pennyslvanian* 8 February 1833, p. 2, bottom col. 2). And a long, empty biography of him is in the New York *Sun*, 12 June 1834, calling him the "terror of evil-doers and little boys."

16. Charles White's adaptation omits this scene, but Rice retained it in his one-act version, and the accounts in playbills confirm that Rice opened Act Two of his full version with it.

17. The one-act prompt script for 1839 specifies "business" here, but does not say what it is. Actors might have kissed, danced, hugged, sung—and all would have been appropriate.

18. Touring actors played benefits before they left town to continue their circuit. On benefit nights they received a higher percentage of the gate. So, Bone is saying he wants to have his benefit before he goes with the Devil. But the saying is a pun, and Bone also hopes to consummate his marriage.

19. This is an early instance among a chain anticipating Rice's performance of Otello's "Farewell, joy, pride, pomp and come riot / Otello's occupation am gone" nearly a decade later. In 1842, at the Adelphi in Edward Stirling's *Yankee Notes for English Circulation*, Rice's character Hickory Dick will misquote Othello: "Julicum Caesar occipation's gone . . . an am neber catch him again—neber." All the up-market critics had been comparing Jim Crow to Othello, but Rice resisted the connection before he bitterly took it on in 1844.

20. The only evidence for this scene is that it exists in the Charles White variants.

Otello

1. *Otello* was not published until 2003. I transcribed and edited the manuscript in the New York Public Library, Billy Rose Collection, call number NCOF +. Dated April 1853, the manuscript says at its top: "Property of John B. Wright copied by permission from the Manuscript of His Friend T. D. Rice, Esq." Born in Newburyport, Massachusetts, 1 October 1814, Wright worked his way up at the Tremont Theatre, beginning as a call boy in 1833 to become its stage manager (Allston T. Brown, *History of the American Stage* [New York: Dick & Fitzgerald, 1870], p. 407). The manuscript also specifies the "Music arranged by Mr. Tyte."

Rice wrote this play. Its text includes remarkable supplements to the Othello story. It is based on the structure of Maurice Dowling's burlesque (Maurice Dowling, *Othello Travestie*, vol. 2 of *Shakespeare Burlesques*, Stanley Wells, 1834 [reprint, Wilmington, Del.: Michael Glazier, 1978]). But the language, the ending, and the progeny differ radically from Dowling's and all other versions of the story that I know.

The first production was at the Philadelphia Chestnut Street Theatre when Francis Wemyss was managing it, 28 October 1844; the cast (according to the Philadelphia *Public Ledger* on the day): Otello, Mr. Rice; Iago, Mr. Jordan; Brabantio, Mr. W. Chapman; Duke of Venice, Mr. Sullivan; Roderigo, Mr. Brunton; Desdemona, Miss H. Mathews; Emilia, Mrs. Hautonville.

2. Nonsense.

3. The dialect here indicates that Iago is summarizing Otello's talk.

4. Mrs. Rowbotham, playing Ninette in *The Bold Dragoons*, sang "Merry Swiss Boy" at the Chestnut Street Theatre in Philadelphia, 12 June 1833.

5. A small coin, as a penny.

6. "Squatulate" is a short form of "absquatulate," or "decamp," "run off."

7. Leave, be off.

8. The devil.

9. This formula for polite racism is Dowling's coinage. Shakespeare has at this point: "Though I do hate him as I do hell's pains, / Yet for necessity of present life, I must show out a flag and sign of love" (1.1.154–156). Dowling has Iago sing it to the air of "Bow, wow, wow": "And though I hate the black blackguard, as I do hate the devil, / I'd cut his throat with pleasure—but I wouldn't be uncivil" (9).

10. Cut, strip, whip.

11. *Gretna Green,* by Lawrence Dromcolloher, was a popular Scottish ballad opera about elopement.

12. Dowling specifies the music as "Follow, Follow." Wright's transcription of Rice's play does not specify the music.

13. This bribe, and the next line confirming its effectiveness, is a touch Rice continues from Dowling; it is one of the many nineteenth-century moves to make the Othello character less the Noble Moor and more a champion among streetwise sparrows.

14. Soaplocks were forelocks that youths created by soaping their hair. They were popular among Bowery b'hoys, one of the first youth cultures that middle-class commentators noticed spawning along the Lower East Side of Manhattan.

15. At the end of his 1.3, Shakespeare gives this racist remark to Brabantio, who says "if such actions may have passage free, / Bondslaves and pagans shall our statesmen be." The idea is not uttered clearly in Dowling's variant; Rice revives it, making it the common sentiment given in chorus.

16. A generally reliable source reports Rice wrote verses to the tune of "'Sitting on a Rail' and dedicated them to Queen Victoria," doubtless at her coronation, when Rice was performing in London (Isaac J. Greenwood, *The Circus* [New York: William Abbatt, 1909], p. 127). By the 1840s, the song was infrequent in Rice's repertoire but "Sitting on a Rail" was popular with other performers. The underlying tune of the council's song is its chorus:

> As I walk out by de light ob de moon
> So merrily singing dis same tune
> I cum across a big raccoon,
> A sittin' on a rail,
> Sittin' on a rail,
> Sittin' on a rail
> I come across a big raccoon,
> A sleepin' wery sound.

In fact, in most of the variants, the song is about the escape of the coon— just as Otello will escape in this scene, and Desdemona will escape later. What does not escape in this song, nor in the play, is ultimate authority. The song figures this authority as the singer's master:

My ole Massa dead and gone
A dose ob poison help him on
De Debil say he funeral song.

The play figures authority as the Duke, Brabantio, and the class that is trying
to judge Otello in this scene. They are bumblers who need the dark hero to
do their business.

17. Shakespeare says "galleys" (1.3); Dowling added the (perhaps
redundant) "slaves." Rice followed Dowling. This addition emphasizes that
the Senate has sent Otello—a former slave—to quell revolutionary slaves.
The shift in attitudes toward slavery in the intervening two and a half
centuries made the nineteenth century players feature this problem.

18. For Shakespeare's "mountebank" and Dowling's "wizard," Rice used
"buzzard." This change is complex and coded. Brabantio clearly means it
grossly negatively; buzzard is worse than crow, a grotesque bird. However, in
the argot of New York's Seventh Ward—where Rice was born and grew
up—a buzzard was a social cleanser that pounced on the society's rotten
matter and bore it away. For instance, at the time Rice was establishing
himself as Jim Crow, a scandal sheet printed in the neighborhood proudly
named itself *The Hawk and Buzzard*. Its mast-head slogan: "Our Gossip Bird
Shall Keep a Bright Look Out And Show the World What Folly Is About."
Their statement of purpose: "We intend to make a St[ate or street?]
inspector of the Buzzard, who will remove every infected carcass from the
City" (*Ely's Hawk and Buzzard*, 1 September 1832). *The Hawk and Buzzard* is
Bone Squash's paper of choice in *Bone Squash Diavolo*. Thus for some in the
audience, to be called a buzzard would be a perverse, if inadvertent,
compliment. There is much inversive irony in the language the authoritative
characters speak in *Otello*.

19. Or, "I'd like to cut his throat."

20. English civil engineer William Cubitt invented the tread mill in 1817
as a machine to punish prisoners.

21. Lashes.

22. Dowling has this speech sung to the tune of "Yankee Doodle." The
Wright MS, however, stipulates "recitative" and the speech that Rice gives
Otello no longer scans to "Yankee Doodle." By 1844, even "Yankee Doodle"
was in some sense inappropriately marked: by then the English had too
often applied "Yankee Doodle" as an essentially *national* air. Rice is opposing
that unity by switching a few lines later to "Ginger Blue," the song named

after his insouciant character in *The Virginia Mummy*. In scene 4, Rice specifies "Yankee Doodle" as the air behind Iago's sarcastic account of the ideal woman—emphasizing Iago's inappropriate clichés.

23. "And no mistake" is a vernacular tic of Bowery b'hoys. Four years later, in his Mose plays, Frank Chanfrau will use it to mark off his knowing characters from the innocents they guide.

24. Ginger Blue was the lead character in Rice's play *The Virginia Mummy*, which he began performing as early as 22 April 1835. But the earliest copyright I have found on the song "Ginger Blue" was 1841, by Richard Pelham, who would become one of the four original members of the Virginia Minstrels in the winter of 1842–1843. How these verses, each a different length, fitted the music is a mystery.

25. All of the black characters that Rice played enjoyed freedom. They were either runaways, like Otello and Jim Crow in *Flight to America,* or were wage servants like Bone Squash in *Bone Squash Diavolo* or Gumbo Chaff in *Oh! Hush!* Dowling's Othello was "an independent Nigger, from the Republic of Hayti."

26. Jail.

27. This is the first mention of what will be a cardinal feature of Rice's variant of the Othello story: Desdemona and Otello have a son that does not appear in Cinthio, Shakespeare, or Dowling. This son is the story's problem child—an objective correlative that flames for the first time the smoldering emotional issues at the story's core.

This moment in which Desdemona reveals her desire and leads on the Othello character is also the spot that most offended elite contemporary commentators on *Othello.* John Quincy Adams attacked Desdemona's forwardness in the *American Monthly Magazine* (March 1836, pp. 209–217), complaining in classic racist terms of a well-bred girl attracted to "the sooty bosom, the thick lips, and the wooly head" of a "blackamoor." James Henry Hackett, who was a star contemporary with Rice and often played in the same theatres with him, wrote in *Notes, Criticisms and Correspondence upon Shakespeare's Plays and Actors* ([1863] New York: Benjamin Blom, 1968), p. 224:

[Desdemona] falls in love and makes a runaway match with a blackamoor, for no better reason than that he has told her a braggart story of his hair-breadth escapes in war. For this, she not only violates her duties to her father, her family, her sex, and her country, but she makes the first advances . . . The blood must circulate briskly in the veins of a young woman, so fascinated, and so coming to the tale of a rude, unbleached African soldier. The great moral lesson of the tragedy of *Othello* is, that black and white blood cannot be intermingled in marriage without a gross outrage upon the laws of Nature; and that, in such violations, Nature will vindicate her laws.

Every aspect of Rice's *Otello* is heightened to call attention to and trouble this racism. For instance, in nearly every instance Dowling's white characters referred to Othello as "rascal" or "wight," Rice changed the epithet to "nigger."

28. Fly Market was at the foot of Maiden Lane in Lower Manhattan; there, New Yorkers sold and bought slaves in the eighteenth century. This part of Desdemona's story was added to Shakespeare's telling by Dowling, to be sung to "Bonnie Laddie." Rice compounds the addition by putting Desdemona's song into its camp call-and-response staging against the slave-market background of the tune. Desdemona's song in Dowling is a solo; the polyphony in Rice's variant multiplies the irony and emphasizes that her attraction to Otello was shared, hardly aberrant. Rice shows a cohort staging an emergent cultural option.

29. This may be the moment of conception, a possible play on immaculate, or unknown, conception. There is good wordplay here with *Great-full* and (*sc*)*rape*. Rice or his copyist changed the conventionally spelled "grateful" in Dowling to this "greatful." If Rice and Dowling are implying a sexual union, and impregnation, they are also admitting a motive for the lovers' hasty, secret elopement. "Scrape" may also refer to abortion.

30. This "*me* just now married," a Dowling coinage, is a vestigial remnant in Rice's text of English Black Stage Dialect, which Rice has generally scrubbed and replaced.

31. Rice used this line also in *Bone Squash Diavolo* (1.1), referring to the devil.

32. Billy Whitlock copyrighted "Miss Lucy Long" in 1842. It is a courting song with overt sexual overtones:

> Take your time, Miss Lucy,
> Take your time, Miss Lucy Long;
> Rock de cradle, Lucy;
> Take your time my dear.

33. Amalgamation was the contemporary term for miscegenation. As John Quincy Adams's and James Henry Hackett's remarks (quoted in note 25) indicate, middle-class conventions abhorred racial mixing. But the practice was, in fact, commonplace in New York's Seventh Ward, where T. D. Rice grew up (see Lhamon, *Raising Cain,* pp. 18–19). Particularly in the way Otello is *singing* the term in a burlesque of a canonical text and inverting conventional expectations of the meaning in the next few lines, Rice indicates his self-conscious reference to the radical form of his play.

34. Money.

35. "Polly Will You Now" was perhaps derived from Gay's *Beggar's Opera,* and its sequel, *Polly.* There is also this intriguing tidbit: "George Rice," wrote Charles White, "a brother of T. D. Rice, was singing a negro song called 'Sing Song, Polly, Won't You Kiss Me, Oh!' in 1837" (clipping from *The World,* titled "Old-Time Minstrels," dated Sunday 20 June 1880, in Rice file at Henry Ransom Humanities Research Center, Austin, Texas). Blues scholar Tony Russell has suggested to me that perhaps this song is the forerunner of the song that some hillbilly singers in the 1920s and 1930s recorded, usually under a title more or less like "King Kong Kitchie Kitchie Ki Me O." The lyrics and cadence match, and the parable hidden in the subject matter is not alien. One can hear a pleasant version of this song, sung by Chubby Parker, on the Harry Smith (ed.) anthology, *American Folk Music, Volume One: Ballads* (Folkways FP 251).

For more information on George Rice, see Dale Cockrell, *Demons of Disorder* (Cambridge, England: Cambridge University Press, 1997), pp. 69–70.

36. Poison.

37. An objective correlative for the sexual passion between Desdemona and Otello, this "problem child" (as my then student June Piscitelli wonderfully called him) makes explicit the theme of transracial and cross-class desire that had smoldered, but never been oxygenated, in all the previous variants of the Othello story. "Young Otello," as this child is called in the playbills, was enacted by "Mast. J. Murray" in August 1852, on the same bill with the first New York dramatization of *Uncle Tom's Cabin,* by Charles W. Taylor, at Purdy's National Theatre (Harvard Theatre Collection, National Theatre Folder). Purdy's was the same theatrical space that abolitionists contested with the youth culture of the 1830s—see Lhamon, *Raising Cain,* pp. 29–32.

38. This famous tune was first printed in the western Atlantic in 1794 by

Benjamin Carr, in Philadelphia (Irving Lowens, *Music and Musicians in Early America* [New York: Norton, 1964], pp. 89–91). Especially early on, it had many folk variants.

39. James Gordon Bennett, one of the leading newspaper entrepreneurs of nineteenth-century New York, was friendly with T. D. Rice and, usually, a fan. His paper was the *New York Herald*, later the *Herald*.

40. Or, *I'll estrange you*.

41. Perhaps inadvertent for "clash of cymbals," perhaps intended, especially given the details immediately to be disclosed.

42. These lines indicate that the child actor was blacked up only on one side of his face; the other side favored Desdemona.

43. This song had been in oral circulation in the United States since the Revolution and appeared in several printed collections throughout the nineteenth century. It was apparently a colonial fife song, probably of Irish origin and perhaps via the English variant, "Brighton Camp" (c. 1715). Commencement ceremonies at West Point Academy featured it in the 1960s. The core of the song as usually performed is the *loss* of a lover that one had once hoped would faithfully wait for a return. (Charles Hamm, *Yesterdays: Popular Song in America* [New York: Norton, 1979], p. 250; David Ewen, *American Popular Songs: From the Revolutionary War to the Present* [New York: Random House, 1966], p. 121; G. Malcolm Laws, Jr., *American Balladry from British Broadsides* [Philadelphia: The American Folklore Society, 1957], pp. 248–249).

Rice's incorporation of this song reverses its mood. Otello has overcome the song's dilemma: he has Desdemona back in his arms. He is as much a hero of renewal and connections as Elvis Presley was a century later when he changed earlier (both black and white) versions of "Mystery Train" so that the final stanza brought his girl back instead of taking her away forever. The whole previous history of that song, like "The Girl I Left Behind Me," was about irrevocable loss of one's love, full stop. (For "Mystery Train," see Greil Marcus, *Mystery Train: Images of America in Rock 'N' Roll Music* [New York: Dutton, 1975], pp. 201–203.)

44. Mrs. Keeley (as Jack Sheppard) and Paul Bedford (as Blueskin) sang the duet "Nix My Dolly Palls Fake Away" in J. B. Buckstone's *Jack Sheppard* at London's Adelphi Theatre in 1839. There were at least eight other versions of this very popular play on London stages alone at the same time.

Herbert Rodwell wrote the music and Harrison Ainsworth the lyrics for *Jack Sheppard*. Their song went through at least fifteen printings by D.

Almaine & Co., Soho Square—as attested on its title page in the Enthoven
Collection's Adelphi folder for 1839. From the beginning, they published the
song with footnotes that translated its patois. In the example below, I have
rendered the original footnotes in brackets. That even the contemporaneous
public required translations indicates the social distance that the song and
performance were designed to cross. Bridging that gap was what such plays
as *Jack Sheppard* and *Otello* were about—for they provided a special bonus
value, a release of energy when the connection was made, that cemented the
cross-class filiations these plays established. Here, then, is part of "Nix My
Dolly Palls Fake Away":

Jack

In a box of the Stone-Jug I was born [in a cell in Newgate],
of a hempen widow [one whose husband has been hanged], the
    kid forlorn.

Blueskin

Fake away

Jack

My noble father, as I've heard say,
was a famous merchant of capers gay [a dancing master]

Blueskin

Nix my dolly palls fake away [Nothing comrades, on! on!] repeat

Chorus

Repeat 4 times . . .

Jack

But I slipp'd my darbies [fetters] one morn in May.
And I gave to the dubs [turnkey] a holiday

Blueskin

Fake away

Jack

And here I am palls merry and free,
A regular rolicking romany

Blueskin

Nix my dolly palls fake away,
nix my dolly palls fake away

Chorus

4 times

Since there is nothing comparable in Shakespeare or in Dowling that Rice was drawing on—the whole song is his addition—he clearly meant to make a point with this beautiful tune. It may be that Rice has Otello sing his "notin' to pay" lyrics at this point to emphasize his likeness to Jack Sheppard's Romany or "gypsy" mood. According to the legends and play, Jack Sheppard was hanged at Tyburn; there is plenty to pay.

45. "Rosin the Bow," or "Rosin the Beau," has mysterious origins. As they did with "Jim Crow," black and white singers swapped "Rosin" back and forth within an American transracial repertoire. Its lyrics are a palimpsest of its many performers. This song was the greatest hit of Old Corn Meal, a black street singer in New Orleans during the 1830s. Moreover, Rice performed a skit based on Old Corn Meal on 23 February 1836 at the American Theatre in New Orleans; perhaps he learned the song directly from the street performer (Henry Kmen, "Old Corn Meal: A Forgotten Urban Negro Folksinger," *Journal of American Folklore* 75, 295 [Jan.–March, 1962]: 31, 33). By the end of the decade, "Old Rosin the Bow" had been published in New Orleans and Boston (Henry Kmen, *Music in New Orleans: The Formative Years, 1791–1841* [Baton Rouge: Louisiana State University Press, 1966], p. 242; S. Foster Damon, *Series of Old American Songs* [Providence: Brown University Library, 1936]). But oral transmission continued to carry the song: Appalachian singer Dick Tillett performed "Old Rosin the Beau" for Frank and Anne Warner in 1972 and 1978. The Warners also suggest an older source in a printed "stall ballad by Ryles of Seven Dials" in London that may trace the song back to the seventeenth century (Anne Warner, *Traditional American Folk Songs* [Syracuse: Syracuse University Press, 1984], p. 361).

David Ewen reports that the tune propelled presidential campaign songs repeatedly between 1840 and 1875. In 1844, the year Rice first performed *Otello*, the Whigs twice used the tune to rhapsodize Henry Clay, their losing candidate. Among Democrats, therefore, the tune would have been immediately associated with the sort of hypocrisy that Iago expresses while singing it here.

46. This explicit reference to black/white substitution is neither in Shakespeare nor Dowling. In assigning Iago the "black is white" line during a song in which he declares his hypocrisy, Rice reemphasizes the phony binary of race. The whole point of such performance is to show that race and other genealogical issues are never divisible into either/or options. The blackface mask, the problem child, and this hypocritical reference by Iago all

show—singly and even more together—that black and white hybridization is a persistent fact that the audience must face just as the performers do.

47. Dowling changed Lodovico to Ludovico; Rice followed.

48. "Corn Cobs" was a folk variant on the early strains of "Yankee Doodle," with a mad refrain:

> Corn Cobs twist your hair
> Cart wheel run round you
> Fiery dragons take you off
> And mortar pestle pound you.

Its lyrics were printed in 1834 and the sheet music in 1836 by Endicott in New York (Damon, *Series of Old American Songs*; Constance Rourke, *American Humor*, ed. W. T. Lhamon, Jr. [Tallahassee: Florida State University Press, 1985], pp. 8, 93, 308). During the 1830s the song became associated with the actor George Handel Hill, who played Down East Yankees—often on the same bills with Rice jumping Jim Crow. But Rice had sung the song as an entr'acte, himself, as early as 2 November 1829 in Cincinnati, at about the same time he was starting to black up (but had not yet fixed his stage persona as black). To have Iago sing this song nails the Ensign as a Yankee rationalist. The lyrics here are an amalgam from Shakespeare, Dowling, and Rice; they have nothing of the Tom o' Bedlam refrain of the folk song—*that* is borne by the tune.

49. Dowling's Iago was Irish; Rice's Iago is a Yankee.

50. At what was probably his first benefit performance ever, on 12 June 1830, Rice sang this song in Louisville.

51. Another vestigial remain of Dowling's English Black Stage English.

52. Dowling had Iago make his explanation to the trite "Believe Me, If All those Endearing Young Charms." Rice instead specified "Long Tail'd Blue," one of the oldest and most popular blackface songs. George Washington Dixon was performing it as early as 1827 in New York City. The title refers to the formal morning coat affected by dandiacal flaneurs. It is particularly appropriate at this juncture in *Otello* because it is about an interracial love triangle in which two lovers, at least one black, court a "white gal":

> And yaller folks call her Sue
> I guess she backed a nigger out
> And swung my long-tail blue.

53. Once again Rice connects Iago to Yankee imagery—Stone Fence alludes to a distinctive feature of New England agriculture. Stone Fence was

also one of the earliest American mixed drinks, made from brandy and cider, and mentioned as early as 1809 by Washington Irving. See William Grimes, *Straight Up or on the Rocks: A Cultural History of American Drink* (New York: Simon & Schuster, 1993), pp. 65 and 63. Dowling's *Othello Travestie* had them drinking ale.

54. The social life of Bowery youths often revolved around the volunteer fire companies that marshaled young men to emergency actions, after which carousing and treating would take place.

55. "Soft sodder" appears also in Dan Emmett's "Bressed Am Dem Dat 'Spects Nuttin'" (Hans Nathan, *Dan Emmett and the Rise of Early Negro Minstrelsy* [Norman: University of Oklahoma Press, 1962], p. 411). Soft solder would seem to be the result of very "hot air" or inauthentic language.

56. This gratuitious slur is not in Dowling. But does it indicate Rice's racism or, perhaps, Desdemona's carelessness? Is it designed to elicit audience sympathy for Otello's growing anger?

57. Rice is paraphrasing Shakespeare's *Othello* (3.3.9); Dowling omitted the passage.

58. The reference is to Shakespeare's *Othello*, 3.3.157.

59. Slang. During the depression of 1837, many small banks issued poorly secured notes of small value. Iago is saying that his purse is worthless, but Cassio was after something more valuable.

60. This metaphor, from falconry, is extended in Shakespeare's text as part of Othello's soliloquy at 3.3.260–279: it refers to releasing a disobedient falcon downwind, thus discouraging its return. Rice has resuscitated this line, which Dowling omits.

61. They are, of course, still on Cyprus; Iago characteristically emphasizes animal sexuality.

62. Slang exclamation of disgust or impatience.

63. The joke that hysterical people's hair stands out had become so conventional in the minstrel show by the mid-1840s that there were "fright wigs" for actors to wear. That they have proved of lasting significance is shown in John Lydon (formerly Johnny Rotten, when he sang in the 1970s punk group, the Sex Pistols) wearing such a neon anti-conk wig in his publicity photos for his late 1990s tour of North America in a frank commodity, called "Filthy Lucre."

64. "Dandy Jim from Caroline" is an old blackface song attributed to several composers, including Old Bull Myers, Silas S. Steele, Cool White (John Hodges), Barney Williams, Dan Emmett, and T. D. Rice. William Mahar has argued that the song may refer to the scandalous behavior and

extreme politics of James Henry Hammond, the "Dandy Jim" of South Carolina government in the 1830s and 1840s ("Black English in Early Blackface Minstrelsy: A New Interpretation of the Sources of Minstrel Show Dialect" *American Quarterly* 37 [Summer 1985]: 283). For more on Hammond, see Drew Gilpin Faust, *James Henry Hammond and the Old South: A Design for Mastery* (Baton Rouge: Louisiana State University Press, 1982).

65. In Shakespeare this towel was a napkin and handkerchief dyed in mummy and embroidered by a two-hundred-year-old Egyptian sibyl. Dowling's parody broadened the handkerchief to a towel and naturalized the Egyptian sibyl as a gypsy named Powell. Rice changed Powell to Cowell, probably as an in-joke alluding to his friends Joe and Sam Cowell, father and son, with whom Rice had acted from Cincinnati to New York. Sam Cowell went on to a further career in the English music hall, mutating from blackface to cockney.

66. Second appearance of the problem child.

67. Dowling specifies "King of the Cannibal Islands" for this music. Rice's stage directions do not indicate which music he wanted.

68. These crow sounds were not in Shakespeare, not in Dowling. They are an association with Rice as Jim Crow, and they are characteristic of the way Rice registered his characters' tense madness at plays' ends; see the conclusion of *Bone Squash.*

69. Desdemona's waking spasm is Rice's addition; it is neither in Shakespeare nor Dowling.

70. More b'hoy jargon.

71. Actually, he did not see the towel; Iago told him about it. This remark is vestigial, from Shakespeare's *Othello,* 4.1.

72. Another of Rice's additions: this brilliant street expression, meaning "he's dead," has no antecedent in earlier variants of the Othello story.

73. "Old Dan Tucker" was probably written by Dan Emmett early in the career of the Virginia Minstrels, which is to say in the winter of 1842.

74. In the spirit of opera.

75. When Rice positions this song, with different words, also at the end of *Flight to America,* he and the play's author, William Leman Rede, specify that its tune was Samuel Arnold's "Finale to Obi."

Information about the parallel but separate celebrations blacks instituted to celebrate independence in the early Republic is admirably developed in David Waldstreicher, *In the Midst of Perpetual Fêtes* (Chapel Hill, University of North Carolina Press for the Omohundro Institute, 1997), pp. 325–337, and in Shane White, "'It Was a Proud Day': African Americans, Festivals, and Parades in the North, 1741–1834," *Journal of American History* (June 1994): 13–50. Also relevant is Frederick Douglass's famous speech "What to the Slave is the Fourth of July?" (Rochester, 5 July 1852), which comments on and instantiates the same tradition.

76. John Wright's manuscript here notes that the performance lasted "1 hour and 20 minutes / Boston Mass / April 1853."

Selected Bibliography

Abbott, Lynn, and Doug Seroff. *Out of Sight: The Rise of African American Popular Music, 1889–1895.* Oxford, Miss.: University Press of Mississippi, 2002.

———. *Ragged But Right: Black Traveling Shows, "Coon Songs," and the Dark Pathway to Blues and Jazz.* Oxford, Miss.: University Press of Mississippi, 2007.

Abrahams, Roger. *Singing the Master: The Emergence of African American Culture in the Plantation South.* New York: Pantheon, 1992.

Albright, Alex. "Scenes from a Dream: (Nearly) Lost Images of Black Entertainers." In *Images of the South,* ed Karl G. Heider, 55–73. Athens: University of Georgia Press, 1993.

———. "Noon Parade and Midnight Ramble." *Good Country People: An Irregular Journal of the Cultures of Eastern North Carolina,* 61–90. Rocky Mount, N.C.: North Carolina Wesleyan College Press, 1995.

Austin, William W. *"Susanna," "Jeanie," and "The Old Folks at Home": The Songs of Stephen C. Foster from His Time to Ours.* 2nd ed. Urbana: University of Illinois Press, 1987.

Bean, Annemarie, and James V. Hatch, eds. *Inside the Minstrel Mask: Read-*

ings in Nineteenth-Century Minstrelsy. Hanover, N.H.: Wesleyan University Press, 1996.

Berlin, Edward A. *King of Ragtime: Scott Joplin and His Era.* New York: Oxford, 1994.

Brown, Allston T. *History of the American Stage.* New York: Dick and Fitzgerald, 1870.

Cantwell, Robert. *Bluegrass Breakdown: The Making of the Old Southern Sound.* Urbana: University of Illinois Press, 1984.

Cockrell, Dale. *Demons of Disorder: Early Blackface Minstrels and Their World.* Cambridge: Cambridge University Press, 1997.

Cook, James W. "Dancing Across the Color Line." *Common-Place* 4, 1 (October 2003): np. http://common-place.org/vol-04/no-01/cook.

Damon, S. Foster. "The Negro in Early American Songsters." *The Papers of the Bibliographical Society of America* 28 (1934): 132–163.

Dowling, Maurice. *Othello Travestie.* In *Shakespeare Burlesques,* vol. 2. Stanley Wells, 1834. Wilmington, Del.: Michael Glazier, 1978.

Ellison, Ralph. "Change the Joke and Slip the Yoke." In *The Collected Essays of Ralph Ellison,* ed. John F. Callahan, 100–112. New York: Modern Library, 1995.

Engle, Gary D. *This Grotesque Essence: Plays from the American Minstrel Stage.* Baton Rouge: Louisiana State University Press, 1978.

Freedland, Michael. *Jolson.* New York: Stein and Day, 1972.

Garber, Marjorie. *Vested Interests: Cross-Dressing and Cultural Anxiety.* New York: Routledge, 1992.

Gates, Henry Louis, Jr. "The Chitlin Circuit." *New Yorker,* February 3, 1997, 44–55.

Handy, W. C. *Blues: An Anthology.* With historical and critical text by Abbe Niles, pictures by Miguel Covarrubiaa, revised by Jerry Silverman, 1926. Reprint with a new introduction by William Ferris. New York: Da Capo, 1990.

———. *Father of the Blues: An Autobiography.* Ed. Arna Bontemps. 1941. New York: Macmillan, 1947.

Huggins, Nathan Irvin. *Harlem Renaissance.* New York: Oxford University Press, 1971.

Jones, Bessie, and Bess Lomax Hawes. *Step It Down: Games, Plays, Songs, and Stories from the African-American Heritage.* New York: Harper and Row, 1972.

Kmen, Henry A. "Old Corn Meal: A Forgotten Urban Negro Folksinger." *Journal of American Folklore* 75, 295 (January–March 1962): 29–34.

————. *Music in New Orleans, 1791–1841.* Baton Rouge: Louisiana State University Press, 1966.

Levine, Lawrence. *Black Culture and Black Consciousness: Afro-American Folk Thought from Slavery to Freedom.* Oxford: Oxford University Press, 1977.

Lhamon, W. T., Jr. *Deliberate Speed: The Origins of a Cultural Style in the American 1950s.* 1990. Cambridge, Mass.: Harvard University Press, 2002.

————. *Raising Cain: Blackface Performance from Jim Crow to Hip Hop.* Cambridge, Mass.: Harvard University Press, 1998.

————. *Jump Jim Crow: Plays, Lyrics, and Street Prose of the First Atlantic Popular Culture.* Cambridge, Mass.: Harvard University Press, 2003.

Lott, Eric. *Love and Theft: Blackface Minstrelsy and the American Working Class.* New York: Oxford University Press, 1993.

Mahar, William J. *Behind the Burnt Cork Mask: Early Blackface Minstrelsy and Antebellum American Popular Culture.* Urbana: University of Illinois Press, 1999.

Nathan, Hans. *Dan Emmett and the Rise of Early Negro Minstrelsy.* Norman: University of Oklahoma Press, 1962.

Ostendorf, Berndt. "Minstrelsy and Early Jazz." *Massachusetts Review* 20 (Autumn 1979): 574–602.

Reynolds, Harry. *Minstrel Memories: The Story of Burnt Cork Minstrelsy in Great Britain from 1836 to 1927.* London: Alston Rivers, 1928.

Rice, Edward Le Roy. *Monarchs of Minstrelsy: From "Daddy" Rice to Date.* New York: Kenny, 1911.

Riis, Thomas L. *Just Before Jazz: Black Musical Theater in New York, 1890–1915.* Washington, D.C.: Smithsonian Institution Press, 1989.

————. *More Than Just Minstrel Shows: The Rise of Black Musical Theater at the Turn of the Century.* Brooklyn: Institute for Studies in American Music, 1992.

Roediger, David R. *The Wages of Whiteness: Race and the Making of the American Working Class.* London: Verso, 1991.

Rogin, Michael. *Blackface, White Noise: Jewish Immigrants in the Hollywood Melting Pot.* Berkeley: University of California Press, 1996.

Rourke, Constance. *American Humor: A Study of the National Character.* 1931. Reprint with an introduction and bibliographical essay by W. T. Lhamon, Jr. Tallahassee: Florida State University Press, 1985.

Sampson, Henry T. *Blacks in Blackface: A Source Book on Early Black Musical Shows.* Metuchen, N.J.: Scarecrow Press, 1980.

————. *The Ghost Walks: A Chronological History of Blacks in Show Business, 1865–1910.* Metuchen, N.J.: Scarecrow Press, 1988.

Saxton, Alexander. "Blackface Minstrelsy and Jacksonian Ideology." *American Quarterly* 27, 1 (1975): 3–28.

Simond, Ike. *Old Slack's Reminiscence and Pocket History of the Colored Profession from 1865 to 1891.* 1892. Reprint with a preface by Francis Lee Utley, introduction by Robert C. Toll. Bowling Green, Ohio: Bowling Green University Popular Press, 1974.

Toll, Robert C. *Blacking up: The Minstrel Show in Nineteenth-Century America.* New York: Oxford University Press, 1974.

White, Shane. "'It Was a Proud Day': African Americans, Festivals, and Parades in the North, 1741–1834." *Journal of American History* (June 1994): 13–50.

Wittke, Carl. *Tambo and Bones: A History of the American Minstrel Stage.* 1930. Westport, Conn.: Greenwood Press, 1968.

Wood, Peter H. "'Gimme de Kneebone Bent': African Body Language and the Evolution of American Dance Forms." In *The Black Tradition in American Modern Dance*, ed. Gerald E. Myers. Durham, N.C.: American Dance Festival, 1988.

Woodward, C. Vann. *The Strange Career of Jim Crow.* 1955. New York: Oxford University Press, 1966.

Zanger, Jules. "The Minstrel Show as Theater of Misrule." *The Quarterly Journal of Speech* 60, 1 (February 1974): 33–38.